HE KEPT ME

JUDE 1:24-25   ISAIAH 43: 1-3

L A D Y   R O B B I N S

WESTBOW
PRESS®
A DIVISION OF THOMAS NELSON
& ZONDERVAN

WestBow Press books may be ordered through booksellers or by contacting:

WestBow Press
A Division of Thomas Nelson & Zondervan
1663 Liberty Drive
Bloomington, IN 47403
www.westbowpress.com
844-714-3454

ISBN: 978-1-6642-3617-2 (sc)
ISBN: 978-1-6642-3616-5 (e)

Print information available on the last page.

WestBow Press rev. date: 07/07/2021

THIS BOOK IS DEDICATED TO ALL THOSE THAT FEEL LIKE THEY CANNOT TELL THEIR STORIES, BECAUSE OF WHO THEIR ASSAILANTS ARE OR WERE. GOD SEES ALL. JUST TRUST HIM.

OFTEN TIMES WHEN WE ARE PROMPTED TO WRITE A BOOK BY THE HOLY SPIRIT ITS TO IMPACT OTHERS THROUGH OUR TESTIMONY. TO ENCOURAGE AND EXEMPLIFY HOW WE ACHIEVED VICTORY IN ALL AREAS OF OUR LIVES THROUGH THE POWER OF GOD. WELL LET ME START OFF BY SAYING "I GIVE GLORY TO THE FATHER, THE SON, AND THE HOLY GHOST, WITHOUT WHOM I WOULDN'T BE HERE TODAY.

AS I BEGAN TO JOT DOWN AND REFLECT ON LIFE'S UPS AND DOWNS, VICTORIES AND TRAGEDIES. DISTINGUISHING REALITY FROM FANTASY. I SHARE WITH YOU THE SOMETIMES HORRIFIC AND DEVASTATING THINGS IN MY LIFE. BUT I WILL CONCLUDE WITH THE *VICTORY I FOUND IN CHRIST JESUS. WHEN I REALIZED THAT HE IS THE MAN WITH MASTER PLAN OF MY LIFE. THE FACT THAT HE KEPT ME THROUGHOUT IT ALL AMAZES ME.* BUT THEN I REALIZE HE MAKES EVERYTHING TO WORK FOR MY GOOD FOR HE CALLED ME ACCORDING TO HIS PURPOSE AND BECAUSE OF THAT, I AM SAVED, DELIVERED, AND SET FREE. *TO ALL THAT READ THIS BOOK I PRAY THAT THE INSPIRATION THAT PURSUED ME DOES SO TO YOU AS WELL.*

MANY PEOPLE ARE OPPRESSED BY PAST HURTS, CHILDHOOD TRAGEDIES, AND EVEN LIFE'S MISTAKES AND WRONG DECISIONS. BUT THE CATALYST TO IT ALL IS *GOD'S LOVE.* IT PROPELS US INTO HIS DIVINE PURPOSE FOR EACH OF OUR LIVES. I PRAY THIS BOOK CHANGES SOMEONE'S PERCEPTION ON "FORGIVENESS".

FATHER GOD, HELP ALL THAT READ THIS BOOK PUT THE STRATEGIES AND TRICKERY OF THE DEVIL TO NOUGHT IN JESUS NAME. WE DECLARE WE ARE MORE THAN CONQUERERS. AND WE HAVE ETERNAL LIFE WITH CHRIST. SO FATHER AS I ARTICULATE, AND CATEGORIZE MY LIFE, LET SOMEBODY KNOW THAT CHRIST IS ALIVE AND IF THEY JUST HOLD ON TO HIS UNCHANGING HAND, THEY WILL MAKE IT. AMEN

GOD IS NO RESPECTER OF PERSONS, BUT HE IS A RESPECTER OF FAITH. SO JUST BELIEVE, WHAT HE DID FOR ME HE'LL DO FOR YOU ALSO.

Contents

Chapter 1   In The Beginning.. 1

Chapter 2   Situation Shift 7

Chapter 3   Shoe on the other foot 15

Chapter 4   Change has Come 21

Chapter 5   Embracing Life 27

Chapter 6   Mine Eyes Has Seen The Glory 35

Chapter 7   Carrying the Mantle 45

Chapter 8   Reflections, Prayers, Encouragement.................................57

Daily Devotional Words 61

1

IN THE BEGINNING

INTRODUCTION
SOMETIMES I DREAD TO THINK BACK ON THESE DAYS OF OLD. THEY
ARE BOTH COLD & DARK. WHILE I WAS JUST A LITTLE GIRL {STILL IN
KINDERGARTEN}. WHEN EVERYONE ELSE WAS PLAYING WITH DOLLS,
GOING TO PARKS, LEARNING THEIR ABC'S AND 123'S, I WAS FORCED INTO
AND ADULT LIFE. YEAH I WAS ENGAGING IN ADULT LIKE ACTIVITIES.

One evening while I was visiting my father, I saw him smoking a cigarette and i became
curious. He'd constantly smoked in my presence, and I thought it was cool. So I decided to
imitate what I'd seen him do numerous times before. Dad went into his bedroom, and left the
cigarette butt in the ashtray. Now this ashtray was a regular ashtray, but to me it seemed as if it
was beckoning me to approach it, so I did. Then I picked up the cigarette placed it to my lips,
as if I was truly smoking. Then I got nervous and quickly put it down. Another time, oh about
3 wks from the first time, I gained courage enough to not only pretend to smoke, but light it as
well. This particular time dad had gone to the store. This is just the beginning. He also smoked
marijuana cigarettes and I somehow fooled myself into trying them a well. Don't fault daddy, he
probably didn't't expect for his precious "baby girl" to do such a thing. In my times of visitation
I found myself outside on several occasions smoking. Yeah it was hard at first, but i persisted
and each week it got easier and easier. One week the neighbor came down the back stairs to the
apartment and questioned me about the stench of marijuana in the air. I quickly replied "I don't
know ma'am". The next week she did the same thing, and my reply remained the same, "I don't

know ma'am". So she asked for my dad. I called him to the door and they began to speak, but the conversation was very brief, dad called me inside the house and that was that. By that time he realized that some of his marijuana (roaches)were missing. He put two and two together and concluded that whatever the neighbor was saying had to be true. I thought I was going to get a whooping, what i got was and invitation to join him. That's where my story begins. Once I engaged in the antics of smoking with him, he'd touch me. No not like a father should touch his own child or any child for that matter, and I was afraid. Never did I cry or try to push him away. So the incest progressed to more than just touching. But I was being compensated for it, with things. Any toy, expensive clothes and shoes, etc. so I kept my mouth shut.

On the other hand, when I was at home with my mom strange things were happening there as well. Mom was usually zoomed or zoomed out, so she couldn't see or distinguish what was happening. Once she told her boyfriend to pick me up from daycare. When he came to get me, he was riding a bicycle so I had to ride on the handle bars. When we got home I rushed to the bathroom, by the time I came out, he was stark naked standing their swinging freely. What was I suppose to do? In fear I tried to run, but he just grabbed me. I shrugged him and he just placed me in a hold I couldn't escape from. He did some nasty things to me including touching me, making me touch him, and pleasing himself in front of me. By this time I was just flabbergasted at what was happening. Finally when mom arrived I told her, and she confronted him, but of course he denied it, called me a liar, said "I was being disobedient so he had to spank me". So she chose to leave it alone. Not more than 4 weeks later after this happened, he was stabbed with a knife in my mom's home. Yes he lived, but it was touch and go for a minute. So I did what any other daughter would do. I told daddy and he was furious. But pause, why? Aren't you doing the same thing? Any how, daddy went to confront him but the guy was so defensive and offensive at the same time that he confused daddy, changed the story and made me to be the blame, stating I was lying. Dad told me if he did it again to let him know. Contrary to your expectations it never did. Thank God. Which tells me that even then God was there. I didn't understand it, but God blocked it, *Hallelujah.*

Six months later I was visiting my father's mother (my grandma) house, and a family member said to me "Tanya sometimes he plays with me". I'm only around 7yrs old at this time, so I was like really! She said "we play hide and seek, but when or if he finds me, then I got to kiss him". Now y'all know how that's not how the game goes, unless you're older maybe. So I was like huh? I asked her "what you mean he makes you kiss him?" She said "no, I have to kiss him because I got out, (lost) I didn't hide in a good place." So we talked a little bit more and I discovered she too was going through it. I was shocked, but then I asked her why did she tell me? She said because my he said you know how to play all our "secret" games. I'm thinking how did he know that? But right there you see it was ok to do it, because it was "usual" or should I say the "norm". So I asked her did you tell your mom?" She was like, yeah she already know.

Yes, this is something in the *bloodline of the males on that side of the family tree that was tolerated.* She was actually trying to recruit me, and I didn't realize it. She never suspected that I too was already going through the same thing. But like me she was being compensated, just as I was. Being deceived into believing it's ok. There was so many female cousins to choose from and she chose me, I wondered why? The answer is "the youngest female child" is who they wanted. So be cautious when you see your girls being *extra* friendly or very open with older men it's a sure sign. At the age of 8, it was my turn to recruit somebody. I was scared, but I knew it was part of "our secret". So I tried my other cousin, she was happy to come and stay with me because she didn't have the things I had. She didn't have the toys I had. It was a new experience for her. So she agreed. But when she asked her mom she was like "I got to think about it". So 1 week go by still no decision, 4 weeks still no definite answer, So I thought I had failed in the task of getting somebody else to experience what I'm going through. This was supposed to be my way of escape. So finally 2 months later her mom said yes. I was so happy, even elated to know I won't be alone. And to my surprise the whole atmosphere changed. usually we'd go to the movies {dad dropping us off}but this time he said "y'all big girls now, go ahead and walk to the theater. Which was about 4 blocks away from where my grandma lived. So of course we were overjoyed. I remember it like it was just yesterday. It was a Saturday, me and my cousin was so anxious to walk to the movies alone, mind you were both 8 and 9 years old, she was older. But I'm smoking marijuana on the regular now every weekend. So I had some with me, that was *the bait.* So as we're walking I showed her and she was like, "where did you get that? Do uncle know you smoke? Of course I didn't disclose any information, I even avoided the question all together by just firing up a spliff. Now to those that don't know this when you get two sheets of rolling papers usually 1.5, and and make one long joint (marijuana cigarette). So we toking it up. I mean we having a jolly good time, {puff puff pass}. When we reach the movies we high as a kite, just giggling and laughing, not really paying attention to the movie. I believe we were going to see Friday the 13th. Back then people were smoking, eating, and doing other things in the theater. So every time a killing scene happened we'd scream like everybody else. We didn't look like the typical 8 and 9 year old kids, we could pass for 13. After the movie we went to Burger King, and that's when she asked me what were going to do at the sleep over? Wow, just like that? I hesitated to answer, then I just said "we gone bake some cookies in my easy bake oven", yeah that's fun. All the while I know something more is going to happen. We get home and I'm expecting for my dad to touch me or her, but to my astonishment he never did. The whole weekend was molestation free!! I dare not question why, I just was relieved.

The final piece to the beginning puzzle is this. Not more than 6 months after I turned 9, my daddy said "instead of going to the movie, or watching a movie, lets make a movie". What, I'm thinking to myself?" Yeah we can make our own movie." So he pulled out the projector and showed me some scenes he wanted to try. But first the pictures, oh my goodness the pictures of me naked, me in compromising positions, me doing some adult things. I mean I was already acting as a porn star, now the day has come that I have to actually be what I'd been watching on tv. I didn't know exactly what to do and how to do it, but I did it. I made a movie, starring me and my daddy, it was recorded on a vhs beta max tape. Then I had to continue taking pictures and allowing him to film me doing things like pretending to perform on fruit. Even touching myself. *The reason I'm being so explicit is I need you to understand how I felt at that moment. I knew that anytime I went to visit daddy, I'd be subject to this activity. So I had to wise up and try something different, because by now I too have accepted this as the "norm".* The purpose of the first chapter is to show you that even if you think the "perfect family" don't have issues, think again. Everything isn't always what it looks like. Yeah I was happy, but I was scared, sad, and confused all at the same time. Although he was my dad and hurting me, I still loved him. This act of molestation and incest usually start around this age. Even if you think something is wrong ask questions. As far as the drug use goes, children often times emulate what they see adults do, especially their parents. I thank God for every experience in this portion of my life. It is the beginning stages of grooming me into who I am today.

In spite of all the things I shared so far, I was also a sickly child. At the age of 2, I was diagnosed with epilepsy. I was in and out of the hospital, sometimes for weeks at a time. Miami Children's Hospital was my home away from home. Even the medication didn't seem to help. I don't recall having any attacks at this tender age, but I know they were happening readily. My parents often had to negotiate who would sit with me at my appointments. Daddy was mainly the one who did. I do remember once while in the hospital daddy brought me a teddy bear to comfort me before I went in for a EEG, EKG, and CAT Scan all in the time period of 5 days. I loved that teddy bear. Then he replaced it with a *cabbage patch doll*. I didn't like that ugly thing. I wanted my teddy bear instead. But eventually I grew to love my baby, she was my friend. I'd talk to her, and squeeze her, hoping the pain and fear would go away. But it didn't.

Granny in the meantime was very keen about little girls and men, males period. She'd often say "don't sit in no man's lap! Or "I better not catch you in no grown ups face!". You know that's a no-no in our culture. But she couldn't see what I was facing at home. Or maybe she did, because often times she favored me. I'd be with her all the time.

I know she was the one that raised me. I lived with her on several occasions. I remember one day when I was younger than "the beginning" ages, maybe 3, and my preschool went to the park on a field trip. And I somehow got left behind. I was so scared. But I didn't panic. Granny (Ma) had taught me how to get home if I ever got lost. She said "first locate an adult, then tell them to call the police, and direct the police officer to your house. I didn't know the address but since the park was so close to my house, the police officer cruised down every street until I recognized my street and could direct him on how to get to my house. *God kept me, it could have been worse, but again God blocked it.* On many occasions I'd go with Ma to work on Indian Creek Island, to help her clean house. She had a normal routine, and when it was time for the stories (soap operas) everything shut down. Afterward we would get on the bus and come home.. she d stop and get her bottle of liquor and me, well like I said she favored me, I'd get Chicken Unlimited, that was the normal when it was her payday. I'm trying to show you how i came to know the Lord, it was grandma. She'd walk around humming hymns and quoting scriptures. She'd take me to church with her. One time we didn't go to our usual church, we went to a new/different church, and the man began preaching and all of a sudden I began to get a funny feeling in my belly. As he continued to talk I understood some of the things he was saying, mind you I'm about 9 or 10. So when the invitation to Christ came I quickly went up. I thought that's what you supposed to do, at least that's what we did at our church. Everybody came to the front together. But at this church it was different. Grandma saw me and she just began to cry. I was scared that I had did something wrong. After service she called me to the side and said "do you know what you did? Why did you go up there?" My answer was "I don't know". She the grabbed me in her arms and embraced me in a way of relief, joy, love, and reassurance all at the same time. On that day, on the way home we went to Burger King, my favorite place. Later that night my Ma said to me "God chose you". I didn't know what that meant but I said okay. This is to help you to understand that God chooses children as well as adults. Even at this tender age I knew of God. There many cases in the Bible where God chose children. David was a teenager when he slew Goliath. Joseph was a child when he was thrown into jail after being sold by his brothers. Mary was a teenager when God chose her to be the mother of *Our Lord and Savior Jesus Christ*. Train up a child in the way they should go, and when they get old they will not depart from it.

2

SITUATION SHIFT

INTRODUCTION

In this chapter some of the old things are still happening. But now they are more intensive. New situations arise to the point of unbelief. But this shifting is both good and bad.

In the fourth grade I was raped on the school crosswalk. Never did I imply or even act as if I was sexually active. But these boys were known for being trouble makers. Everybody was afraid of them. You know this is usually the age when we begin to mature physically, but I had already done that. I had the physical appearance of a 12 or 13 year old at 9. I had breast and curves. One of the boys asked me to be his girlfriend. I said no! He continued to pursue and harass me for 2 weeks. He'd shove me, {you know that's a courting tactic at this age}he'd write notes, and follow me around the school, so he knew my route. Many girls were raped on this catwalk, but no one ever came forth to say who it was. Finally I told the boy okay I'll be your girlfriend. He immediately got in a huddle with his friends. Next day on my way home, I took the same route as always, but this time "my boyfriend", said "wait a minute, don't go up there yet, so I stayed on the spiral part of the cross walk, between the stairs on the side of it and the actual crosswalk over the street. In about five minutes time he came back and said "come on let's go". I didn't have a clue what was waiting for me around the bend. When I was just about to enter the main part of the crosswalk, I was approached by two of the other guys. They demanded that I have sexual relations with them, or I couldn't go to the other side. It was more like they were charging me a *toll charge* to cross. I refused, and they got even more aggressive. I turned to see where my "boyfriend" was, and he standing there with his pants down. I tried to escape, but mind you I really have no where to go, I'm stuck. Then they all say "if you say anything, it'll be your last words". So now I'm passed scared, I'm terrified. As each of them had their way with me. I cried profusely. After they finished the made sure to reiterate, "if I told anyone anything, those would be the last words I ever spoke". So I just waited until I thought they were gone, and then I proceeded to cross the crosswalk. I was so angry, yet ashamed so no I didn't tell a soul. This type of behavior was always happening on this crosswalk. Thank God, three days later another victim went to the principal and told what happened to her. And it was at that point when they announced not to use that particular crosswalk anymore. Investigations were done, but they were never pointed out. The young lady never said who it was neither did I, although we knew them personally. Besides, I was just glad that something happened to prevent it from happening again. Now I'm in my late stages of 10 years old and I'm introduced to a new thing, *powdered cocaine*. Daddy was now a dealer, not regular five and dime bags, not even $20 bags. No, he was dispensing weight. Minimal quantities *eight balls*. You're probably asking why didn't you tell your dad about those guys? Well like I said I was scared of them. We all lived in the same neighborhood and their reputation's were fierce. In fact their whole family was known to be bullies. I wanted no parts of them.

I'd still visit daddy on a regular, but now I'm spending more time with him. He's picking me up from school now. This is my junior high school years. My first year in 5th grade. Here's where I remember the seizures coming about. I was in P.E. class, and we had to do warm ups before we could play or participate in the class activities. I was in the locker room getting *dressed out*, and I felt sick. I didn't know what to do or say. I just told my teacher Ms. King, I had to go home. She said "what's wrong", I said "I don't feel good", she said "young lady finish getting dressed and come out of here", I said "Ms. King, I'm sick". That's all I remember, from that point my schedule was changed. I no longer had P.E. anymore, instead I had "strings" (music education). One day as we were in our homeroom class, there was a boy crushing on me. I knew this boy's reputation, which was good. All the girls wanted to be his "girl friend", yeah including me. So we flirted and wrote notes back and forth until it was obvious to others we were boyfriend and girlfriend. Other girls were jealous and envious of this. I mean I had to fight on several occasions just because of the fact they didn't like that I was his girlfriend.

During the summer of my 5th grade year, I was again asked to invite my cousin to spend the weekend with me. This time I was seduced into doing it. I mean I was laying in "our bed" {rarely did I sleep in mine}and the conversation of what kind of of bed do you want arose. It's time to upgrade your room. So I said "I want a water bed", dad replied "are you sure?" Yes I said, and I need lots of stuffed animals to go with it. Why a water bed, he asked? I said, I wanted one like yours with radio in the headboard. Really, he hopped up, so he said, "we'll first look for one like mine, and if we can't find one, we'll get the water bed, ok. The next day the people were delivering my brand new water bed. And I went out and purchased new cabbage patch dolls, Care Bears. . I got to finally participate in a "white party" {cocaine distribution and use}. I wasn't out front, but I was in the room secluded. I had my own supply of weed and coke, and Burger King too, I was satisfied. Dad's instructions was "do not come out of this room". So I complied willingly. After the people left I was compensated in other ways as well. {again my explicitness is to bring you into my mindset not to offend}I was all in for recruiting of my cousin. I called her and asked her to come over, but now she's living with her aunt because her mother was murdered over some dirty money. So at first she was very leery about asking her aunt. One week later she called me and said her auntie said yes, so I was filled with joy. She had no idea what had occurred within the time we'd been apart. How I now had elevated my drug use both type and quantity. Any how we went to pick her up, and she was looking frazzled in her face, so I asked her what was wrong? She said "my aunt said, if uncle was around we should stay in the room". Mind you this is the same cousin I recruited before, so I thought. By the time we get home she'd calm down and was glad to be with me. More like sisters than cousins again. I opened the door to my room and she gasped, standing there with her mouth opened for about 2 minutes. Then she finally said "ooh cousin you got a water bed". I replied, yeah. And she plopped down on the bed. We didn't realize then that you not supposed to plop down on a water bed. I'd never slept in it anyhow. So by the next morning the bed seemed a little different but we didn't think nothing of it. She called her auntie as she was directed to do every morning and check in. Her aunt asked was she ok, I'm looking like why did she asked that silly question. Cousin answers yes ma'am. I go to fix us some cereal in the kitchen, and daddy asked are y'all ok, I'm looking puzzled at him, yes I reply. Neither me or my cousin knew that my dad and her aunt had already spoken on the phone the night before on the count of the aunt being leery of dad. Apparently it had already been said that people had suspected my dad and his brother of being sexually abusive or molesting their girls, due to the fact that our relationships with our father's were too close for comfort. To some they were just down rite unusual. So I went back to the room and everything seemed well. No smoking, occurred. Nor did any sexual advances. Again I'm like why is he telling me to get her to come over but nothing happens in her presence. I just couldn't understand that. Later that evening we looked at the bed and it was lower than before, and we noticed water on the other side of the room. She got scared. I told her don't worry, its ok. She was afraid that we would get in trouble, she began to panic, she started hyper ventilating, pacing the floor, so I just did what I thought was best, I told dad. I showed him and the problem was solved. The next day her aunt called and she (my cousin) was crying on the phone. I asked her again what was the matter she said she had to go home. Her aunt insisted that she come home immediately, so we obliged and took her home, I never understood why? As a matter of fact she couldn't ever be my slumber partner anymore. God Blocked It. Me being lonely would often say to myself "what did I do?" Maybe she felt she did something wrong? I just couldn't't figure it out.

Now its time to go back to school, and I am still Anthony's girlfriend. Then tragedy strikes. While were going to lunch. We lined up as normal to go down the back stairs and Anthony decided to go ahead to the next set of stairs. Mind you we are on the third floor. He decided to slide down the banister railings and his shoe laces got stuck. He tried to pull them out, but he pulled a little too hard and he fell from the third floor to the first floor right in the middle of the school, "splat", there he was dead. We all were just devastated, we couldn't believe what we had just seen. They quickly whisked us away to our class, and dismissed us about two hours later. We had just seen a fellow student plummet to his death. School closed for the remainder of the week and counseling was offered. On the day of the funeral, we "Ms. McDonald's 5th grade class" wrote notes in memory of him and gave them to his family.

My mom's drug use is getting worse. She's now going with the neighbor. This man was the epitome of a pervert. He'd feel on me when she'd send me to ask him for sugar. He'd feel on me if I was walking by his door, he'd try and touch me when he'd come to the house, it was like there was no escape from him. One day mom had left and I had to use his phone to call my dad, this man literally put his hands up my dress. I couldn't do nothing but cry. When daddy got there I told him I wanted to move with him. Besides I didn't want to go to that same school anymore. So he said we'll see. Nothing happened for a while. Mr. Robert continued in his daily attempts to grope, touch, feel, and even give sexual gestures with his tongue. "Ewww" just thinking about this turns my stomach. Thank God I had a way of escape.

My best friend would call me over to play with her. She lived with her grandma at the time. She like me was very spoiled, {she's an only child}. I never knew why she lived with her grandma. I know she despised her mother. Ms. Hilda would Burger King and Jumbo us so much that I'd be full at dinner time. I stayed over with her on many occasions. We were inseparable. She went to private school, so I asked my dad could I go to her school. We went and applied and I got in. I believe I attended that school for about four months. I forgot why, but I went back to my old school. When I returned back to my old school, it was around the the time of the pouring in of the immigrants, especially the Haitians in the USA, specifically in Miami. Well one of my friends Marie was being bullied because of her weight, how she looked, her nationality, you name it, she was being picked on for it. Now Marie, Tanya, Venice, and I were a group of four that bonded like gorilla glue. Marie would rush home from school to catch "Days Of Our Lives", and she wouldn't miss an episode. She knew all the characters names and everything at the age of 11. One day on of the school bullies "called her out", she was scared. So I stepped in and said she'll be there. After school that day Marie didn't show up right away, when she did immediately the bully went after her. I barged in and said fight me, so the crowd was amped up, I was hyped up, and the fight was on. It seemed like forever because although we started fighting down the street from the school we continued fighting until we got about a block and a half further. How we stop I don't know, but I tell you what, Marie never had any more problems after that. Another occasion of me fighting for the underdog is when my classmate Kelina Ducatel was being bullied for being adopted. The kids would single her out and just make her cry. I told her "don't listen to them", I even began calling her my sister. Uh oh, now see you messin with my family. When they came at her again I "called them out". After school I was looking for them but they were no where to be found. We went to the store, normal routine after school, and there they were. But they didn't want to fight. Kelina lived around the corner from them so I had to make sure she got home safe. Don't you know they waited until they got on their block and got "all puffed up". It was two sisters. These same two sisters I had trouble with before because the little one didn't like that I was Anthony's girlfriend. So first Kim, the older one made an advance as if I was gone be scared of her. She didn't know me very well. so I was like what you gone do? Then Shonda, the younger one got her confidence up as soon as we approach their house. She began running her mouth, mind you, I got to get Kelina home safely, so I just kept walking, but then she (Shonda) put her hands on me, so there it was, my pass way and it was on. Her momma came out like she didn't see what happened. So we stopped on the account of her mom. But Kim, had to go around the corner, so as I'm walking with Kelina, to get her home safely I run into Kim again and she confronts me, then here I go fighting her. It was actually Anthony's mother that broke us up.

We got news that My dad's mom had passed. I vaguely remember her, but I do remember her speaking to me in a dream afterwards. She said "baby if you live by the sword you'll die by the sword". The time of her funeral dad was so anxious to get to the ceremony that he told me if I wasn't ready he was going to leave me. The day of the funeral dad came and I wasn't ready. Oh my, this is the first time dad ever showed any kind of disciplinary action towards me. He said "I'll wait 10 minutes then I'm leaving. I must have been more than 10 minutes because when I came out the door he was pulling off. I yelled and he stopped, I tried to get in the car but dad would not let me. So I'm like he just pretending. I am determined to go, but dad would not open the car door. As a matter of fact dad drove with me hanging on the side of the car for about half a block. Then I finally realized he wasn't letting me go, he's really serious. But wait a minute you just made me look like a fool dragging me down the street in my pretty dress. Oh the shame, I felt, let alone the disgrace, disappointment, and anger. No he didn't I thought to myself. So I ran home got in my closet and stayed there until my mom came home and found me. She said why didn't you go with your daddy? I said, he wouldn't let me go, he left me. But then I started crying even harder and louder. She said, what's wrong with you? I said, "he be touching me", yeah I was mad. She said who your daddy? I said "yes". Come here baby, she said. I'll talk to him. But when time to confront him came I recanted what I said. I insisted that I told a lie because I was mad. Did she ever question him about it, I don't know.

Now its my 6th grade year and things are shifting. I move in with daddy permanently. And now I'm changing schools. Grandma's boyfriend is bootlegging alcohol, numbers, cigarettes, you name it. That was usual in those days. He had several friends that would come over to mom's house on the regular. When I'd visit mom, I had to put up with them touching me. One Saturday morning about 11:00am, Mr. Sarge the oldest one came to purchase some liquor. So I took his money, but he insisted to push his way in the door, and proceeded to fondle me for the first time. So I shrugged him in astonishment. I was thinking to myself "did that just really happen? So the next week I came over he did the same thing. I made up my mind to put a stop to this. So when Mr Sarge attempted to touch me again, I pushed him in a way to let him know "this ain't what you want". You'd think that'd cause him to stop. No, as a matter of fact he became a little more aggressive in his attempts. Blocking me from leaving the room, cornering me in an isolated space. So I just stop selling to him. The thing is if you buy at the house you can consume it at the house. And he'd get so drunk he'd forget where he was, so often times he slept over.

Another culture norm "*friends of the family*", people that are close to family members that you should be able to trust. Well we had several of **them**. One name Mr. Deek, this old man groped girls in the open, and everyone knew of it. He didn't care that he was a deacon at the church. He still touched "any" girl he came in contact with. We had a family home and Mr. Deek lived in the back house. So he would come to the main house on several occasions and mingle with family. If we saw Mr. Deek, we'd know to not go around him. But he persisted on getting us, the little girls in his vicinity someway somehow. My cousins Debbie and Kim along with their mother moved in the back house with Mr. Deek, they had nowhere to go, after all they were family. Now these two girls were not blood cousins, *"friend of the family* cousins." Mr. Deek's brother, asked him to house them temporarily. Now I know these girls were being subject to nonstop molestation and harassment by Mr. Deek, but like I was being compensated by my dad, they too were being compensated by Mr. Deek. Now Debbie was the oldest, she'd be in the room with Mr. Deek for twenty minutes or so, then come out and say "Kim, Deek want you. Now those words are very scary to someone that doesn't know what's happening, but somehow, I believe they knew that I was aware of what was going on, because although they were not open about it, they sure did give a lot of subtle hints and gestures. Mind you I haven't said much about their mother, she was rarely there. So these two girls had to fend for themselves. They'd have parties, sleepovers, I mean they were just lose. Here I am trying to fit in because I had no big sisters, so I considered them mine.

One day while working the front "selling the alcohol", Mr. Sarge touched me, and I slapped him. Then my grandma's boyfriend walk in right after, and for the first time he touched me, I was shocked, so I just brushed it off as maybe I imagined that. But the next day while I was working the front again he (grandma's boyfriend) secluded me in the room as I went to retrieve the "shots" ordered, pushed me on the bed and tried to climb on top of me. I kneed him in the groin and ran to my grandma. No I didn't say nothin' but she could tell something wasn't right.

You know them old women had an eye (a discernment) for things like that. But wait can we get a head count right quick, daddy, Robert, Oscar, 3 boys, Mr. Sarge, Mr. Deek, Ma's boyfriend all these males have invaded my personal space on a regular basis. Imagine all of this at the age of 12 and I haven't event started my period yet. I haven't officially changed schools. I'm still at Edison Middle, and I get a very eerie feeling in my stomach. It's the end of the school day, so I rush home to Ma's house {I'd usually go there until dad picked me up}. I go into the bathroom and blood is everywhere. I panic. I call Ma and tell her, Me: "Ma, I'm bleeding, Grandma: Where baby? Me: down there, Ma: Is it a little or a lot?, Me: It's a lot, Ma: Oh baby you just got your period; take a shower, and get some tissue and place it in your panties, and I'll see you when I get home, Me: OK. At thirteen I was still not promiscuous. I was known for my quiet personality. Not shy, just very evasive at times.

Tanya knew of an older girl named Renee, we called her Missy, she usually did the plaits and braids in the neighborhood. By this time we were all sneaking around smoking marijuana on the wall. "The wall" was the meeting place of the neighborhood, and it was directly behind my mom's house. How she didn't catch us still baffles me. One day while at Missy's house everybody showed off their tattoos and were contemplating getting more. Missy was the one doing them. I didn't have any, and was afraid of getting one. But Tanya had one, and she convinced me it wouldn't hurt if I got one. She began to lay out the process:

1st- drink some will I run, (Wild Irish Rose)
2nd- hit a joint,
3rd- Missy would take a safety pin with some Indian ink and tattoo your body (where ever you prefer).

All seemed harmless so I agreed. I tell you steps 1 and 2 should have been joined together, because as soon as Missy fired up the joint and poured the drink, she immediately proceeded to step 3, I saw her burning the pin, and I said "wait a minute, I'm not ready yet" but of course I'm talking to myself, because I don't want to look like a chicken in front of everybody. But Missy was smart, she sensed something wasn't right so she fired up another joint (marijuana cigarette), after 3 or 4 of them and a half a bottle of W.I.R. (Wild Irish Rose) I was brave enough to muster up "some" courage, emphasis on "some." O.K., I got the tattoo but its nothing to brag about, its not my name, nor is it some fancy picture, I couldn't even say its my initials remember I emphasized "some" courage, just enough to get a vertical line for the letter "T", by the time the horizontal line came I was out. So yes, I did my initiation for the block. That's pretty much what it was anyhow.

This chapter is a reminder, that the things we see kids do now we too did, but the difference is, we did it secretly in fear of repercussions. Kids now do everything and anything without remorse or regret and expect us to be ok with it. Remind them I've done that, I just want to spare you the pain. God is good at allowing us to look back and see what could have been. But also be reminded that God blocked it, He wouldn't let it be so. So as things shifted in my life some good some bad, it's now time for me to take control. So now in many aspects the power will be reversed to my advantage.

3

SHOE ON THE OTHER FOOT

Introduction

By now I'm thinking again of changing schools. But just before I officially changed schools another one of my friends passed. I had also now began to act out due to all the molestation and incest. I attempted suicide on several occasions. I took pills over and over, I tried mixing drugs and alcohol, but it didn't work. Eventually my creative writing teacher Ms. Bellamy noticed something different about me. She said something to the principal and he called my parents. They scheduled Ann appointment for a psychiatrist (head doctor, shrink) to figure out what was wrong. My over protective behavior of my friends, or anyone who couldn't protect themselves put up a red flag. So I went to Dr. Isom, accompanied by my daddy one Thursday afternoon. This man probed and primed but I wouldn't budge. Of course I ain't telling nobody what I'm going through. They just might blame me and I'd get trouble, arrest my my daddy or even worse, say I had to go back and stay with my momma, remember I'm trying to run from this already. So Dr. Isom asked questions and I gave him retroactive answers. You see, even at this tender age I was smarter and wiser than all can understand. He, Dr. Isom that is, told my daddy he couldn't detect nothing wrong or peculiar. Success yes, I did it. This clarified I now was capable of being cunning and manipulative.

So now everyone that was causing me any pain, hurt, or discomfort, I now made up in my mind they would pay one way or the other. Starting with daddy, yeah he was spoiling me but now he wanted to go more in depth with it.

Now if he wants to continue doing this, he had to pay and the price just got higher and higher as the acts got more and more explicit. Then one afternoon after I had hung the clothes on the line to dry, and picked a couple limes and lemons to make some drinks to go with dinner. Daddy actually did rape (I did not agree to this act) me. He forcefully backdoored me (sexually assaulted me by sodomy) this I'll never understand why? Even now as I'm describing this I'm getting flustered. My heart is beating fast, I'm trying to breathe. Oh God, this was an extreme insult. When he had finished he said "this is my favorite position". I tell you I cried, I cried, I cried all night long. But I wouldn't tell a soul but God. Because even though I was intensely angry, I loved my daddy. He knew he had hurt me, not just physically but in other ways too, because the next week he booked a trip to Disney World, as if to say I'm sorry. And yes I fell for it.

At 14 years old I was selling drugs on my mom's end. Meaning, when I'd go to visit her, I was selling drugs. I was working for the Big Boyz, not no on the corner type of stuff. I was surrounded by so many different type of chemicals; Oh but God. My mom didn't have to worry about paying for her drugs, I had her. Then I call myself liking one of the Bosses, he liked me too, but of course I'm only 14 years old and he was far pass my age. By now I'm now what the old folks called "one of them fast tailed girls", but I wasn't having sex with any of them. I could demand "double scale" of the drugs without repercussions, so yes I kept mom well supplied. As I was working one evening, I got up to check on something and someone shot up the house and killed my boyfriend, so yeah drive by shootings are real I've been in a couple of them. But God blocked it, nothing happened to me.

On an early school morning I got dressed to go to school with my uniform clothes on. I headed down the street to the bus stop and once reached I changed my clothes. You see we had the choice to wear uniforms or not. So daddy said "uniforms" and I said "not". I wasn't the only one doing this wardrobe change, several girls in the neighborhood was doing it. Just before its time to return home in the afternoon we'd change back as if nothing happened.

Now daddy did have girlfriends. But I was jealous, both as a daughter and get this a "girl friend." When they'd come over I'd pretend to be sick. One lady, knew something was up. Every time she came around I'd interrupt them, walking in and out of the room, I'd come knocking on the door for nothing, making up all types of things. I remember I told daddy I couldn't sleep because the lights from the dog track were coming in my room through the window. He said, go sleep on the couch. I came back and claimed the channels were not working, dad came to fix that, and just before he went back into the room I did the ultimate thing, I faked a seizure, causing her to have leave. That's right lady this is "my man" I said to myself. Of course I had to do what she might have done, but I didn't care. The sexual encounters with my dad so normal now. Like daily it didn't matter. One of his friends (female friends) said to him "your daughter is your wife", it may as well been so, I was doing everything a wife would do, cooking, cleaning, sexing, caring for, putting the bills together, and spending the money, so yes **I was my daddy's**

wife. But it wasn't officially stated until I turned 16. While I was 15, it was decided that I should be homeschooled due to my sickness. After all I was missing so many days anyhow. .

Now on mom's side of town I had a man eyeing me. This man was called "the anything man", ice cream truck driver. And anytime I was around my grandma's house he would stop and talk to me. Free ice cream for the neighborhood y'all. Well this man asked me what would he have to do to prove he was seriously liking me? Well I had high standards, I mean remember I'm a spoiled daddy's little girl, so I said "buy me a house". And he bought the duplex on the corner of grandma's block. What am I gonna do with this? Everybody was astonished by this. But me, I was like I don't want that so I gave it to my sister to do whatever she wanted to with it. He was lavishing me with these type of gifts just to talk to me, but I wouldn't give him the time of day.

The age of 15 was a turning point for me. I was working (no not fast food) but at the clinic. God is good. I started out as a candy striper and got hired permanently. Then came the second job. AIDS was so new, but it was epidemic. I was offered a part time job at the AIDS Awareness Foundation of Miami as a child care worker. So I was working Jessie Trice, AIDS Foundation, and slinging, when did I have a moment to rest. I was also a "wife". As for all those that were molesting me in the beginning, I wasn't going out like that no more. Then there was the twist that occurred. Debbie and Kim now we're contemplating getting their own place. And me as their little cousin wanted to be apart of this grown up decision. They were like my older sisters. So I lived with them almost 6 months, and seen things you couldn't imagine. The place where we lived was notorious for being the place where people go missing. And I seen it to be so. Now Debbie and Kim were hooked up with some shady folks. We partied all the time. Relentlessly drinking and smoking day in and out. But one thing that stood out with my time with them is this, although they were into "everything", they didn't allow it to come to me. They respected me, and protected me from going deeper. God was working through them. He kept from it. Why aren't you at your dad's you may be asking? Well I call myself venturing out. Ok, I got what the old folks call "grown", and left. That's why.... But then tragically Kim died. It's ironic that she died of AIDS, and I worked for the association, and her mom passed from the same thing. This was devastating to Debbie and to me as well. We could no longer live in the apartment, so first Debbie moved out and maybe a week or so later I followed. Where did I go? Back to daddy of course. But I began to notice changes in him. His sexual appetite and aggression towards me was much more calmer. So I just thought that he had met somebody that had taken my place. By this I mean, he finally found a true wife. Well to my surprise it wasn't that. Daddy's drug habit had surpassed what I knew about.

I met a young man Dante, and I'd sneak him in the house after daddy would go to work at night. Being that our neighborhood had a watch committee in place, I did so very carefully. Soon as daddy left for work I'd have Dante wait 10 min, then I'd beep him on his beeper, alerting him all is clear, and he'd come to the back door which was left open for him to come in. Daddy isn't doing everything he used to do, so now my sexual appetite is high. So to answer your question, yes I am sleeping with Dante. He's the only one at this time besides my daddy that I willfully slept with. Back then we had ON T.V. and the Playboy channel, sometimes you can get them on regular t.v. With a lil fuzz, we'd watch that to get us in the mood. Then just before it was time for daddy to come check on me. I'd tell Dante go over to the dog track parking lot. We know when he was coming, 'cause you could hear the the truck coming down the road. Daddy came in check my room, I pretended to be asleep, he'd fix him a lunch, all appeared good, so he'd leave. No sooner I'd beep Dante again to return, as dawn was breaking, Dante would leave not more than 15 min, before daddy would be turning the keys to the lock in the door. Call me lucky or as I've come to say God blocked it. Now there was one boy who liked me, we went to same school together, and he lived 3 houses down from me. But I didn't' like him, besides I had Dante. No, Dante was not a student. You're probably saying you're back in school again. yeah, I wanted to participate in all the things of "high school". I wanted to go to the prom, I wanted to walk with the seniors, I wanted to experience seniors week, all those types of things. So I coerced daddy to let me go back to public school. I started at the high school near mom, so daddy could pick me up after school. But that didn't workout. The janitor at the school molested me, he pushed me in a closet, and ran his fingers down my blouse, and proceeded to touch my snatch-box, for lack of a better terms. He then covered my mouth and fondled himself until he ejaculated. That experience was traumatizing, and embarrassing. I told daddy and we sued the school board, but of course, they flipped it as if I enticed him. Yeah we got the money, but the shame that came along with it. No one should have to feel like they are cause of their own trauma.... I had to transfer schools. So its at my new school, I met Dante. We left off campus for lunch one day and he drove up next to us as we were walking back to school, trying to make small talk, I paid no attention to him. Maybe two weeks later, while waiting for the school bus to come he offered to take me home, and we became boyfriend and girlfriend. Because he was consistent with his pursuit, I responded. So now let's get back to the boy down the street. He figured he'd tell my daddy I was sneaking Dante in the house, he even went on to tell him that Dante takes me to school instead of me riding the school bus. Daddy questioned me and of course I denied it. I said "daddy he just mad because I wont talk to him". But then the neighbor corroborated his story, um hm, that's just how I looked. Oh my goodness what am i going to do now? One night daddy tried to see for his self, he pretended to go to work. How do you know he pretended? When I beeped Dante he said your daddy's car is around the corner. So that night daddy didn't' see no funny business. But as a precaution daddy started locking the back door, where I couldn't get out. And fixing the fence a certain way to tell if it had been tampered with. I guess he was becoming jealous as a husband, or just being that over protective father, I'll never know. So now I had to come up with another way of getting Dante in. It was 4th of July and daddy was teaching me how to use a gun. So that evening we went into the back yard and daddy handed me a 22, and said point it straight up and shoot. I did just that with no problem. Then he handed me a 38, and said "with this one you might need both hands", and I complied, all was well. But this next one 357, I tell just looking at it made me tremble. Daddy was firing his 45, followed by the 44, he said "alright this is the last shot baby girl". Why did daddy take the time to show me all of his auxiliary, maybe as a warning but that didn't stop me. After that we had dinner and dad got dressed for work. Post office open everyday. But I noticed the window in bedroom looked different then the others did. The locks were broader. I immediately went and checked my room, not the same, kitchen not the same, usually its the bathroom that have different windows. Daddy had changed the windows, but the front window in the bedroom was left alone. Uh Oh, my new way. Daddy left for work. I was anxious to see if my presumptions were true. So I signaled Dante and he came, I instructed him to pull the screen out, and come in through the window, it worked. Just as before we were in each other's arms. Now I never told Dante anything about what daddy was doing. I didn't smoke around him. I was innocent, green, lil Tanyka. Dante's visits became less and less because I was having seizures more frequently.

Now my working at Jessie Trice Center tenure was now about up, and the AIDS foundation was going into another type of sponsorship which didn't allow teens to work. Now at 16 as I said it was made official I was daddy's wife, sealed with a ring. Daddy was teaching me how to drive now. Usually he'd be in the car with me, but one time I decided to teach myself. Daddy was asleep, so I got the keys and proceeded to go to the carport. I unchained the gate, got in the car (daddy loved his Cadillac), I put it in reverse, backed up, then in drive, and moved forward. This is what daddy had taught me to do, I did that about two to three times, its that third time. Instead of reverse I put the car in drive and floored the gas pedal, WHAM, the car hit the concrete wall. My mind is not on am I hurt. Its on what am I gone do? I know, I'll pull my "daddy's little girl card", that wasn't working, so I tried "the wife card", not helping, ok, I know, I pulled my "I'm sick card" I started convulsing and shaking, which made daddy forget about the damage to the car. Later the car was repaired and I apologized to daddy. But even here God kept me. Though this chapter is my liaison from childhood into adulthood in my mind. I'm still a teenager. But as you see age has no bearings on wisdom. But deceitful wisdom is just folly. I was foolish in many of my endeavors but God still blocked it.

This chapter is also meant to encourage girls, women, and even boys and men, that manipulation can lead to devastation. Keep watch over your children. Guard your homes. And protect the innocence and integrity of your youth. It is called the Shoe Is On The Other Foot because I thought I was an adult making adult decisions. But in actuality I was a child making childish mistakes. Now a change is about to come, rectifying my actions and thoughts. In this change many lives will be influenced and affected.

4

CHANGE HAS COME

This will be the most effective chapter. Lives will be changed in many ways.

Introduction

At the age of 16 my daddy called me his wife. As I too called him me husband. On my 16th birthday daddy asked me what did I want for my birthday, I replied a car. He said O.K. and what else, I replied "I want to try crack", daddy being my husband said WHAT???? Two days later in the carport was a baby blue Chrysler Lebanon Convertible.

Oh Wow, I exclaimed, is this mine, yes daddy replied. Now I don't need Dante to take me to school, I could drive myself. So for bout 2 months my car was my everything. Rarely was I visiting mom. Besides my siblings were in foster care. I didn't know what was going on over there really anyway. I would pick up my best friend for school, we went to homeroom, then leave. Go and hang out at the mall, the beach, her house, just carelessly following a daily routine for the week. Then on the weekend we'd chill some more. But then one evening I asked daddy, "what about my other gift" you remember I said I wanted to try "crack", daddy looked at me with a look I've never seen before, and he swallowed. Finally he asked me oh you were serious? Yes, I said with remorse. O.K. Let me make some arrangements he said. The next day, I'd seen it done. I knew the authority my daddy had. Daddy made it happen, he got exactly what his "baby girl/ wife" demanded. I have never really experienced this, remember up unto now all I was doing was smoking marijuana and snorting powdered cocaine. But this is something far greater than that. Apparently daddy had a crash course on how to do it. He took the empty beer can pricked holes in it, placed the crystallized rocks on the top an set it ablaze, while inhaling after a few seconds he exhaled, and the smoke trickled out of his nostrils and mouth. I ask him how he felt, he just said "I'm good. Like I said I had never done this before. So I'm looking for after effects. Yeah I was the one that asked, but now I'm scared, its my turn, you know how many people die from just trying this stuff. Then there are those that get addicted, perfect example my mom was an addict. Here I am eager to try it. So here I go, I placed the rocks on the can and I did what I'd seen daddy do, and began to cough and choke, so he took it from me. Maybe an hour later I said "daddy let me try it again", I was determined to do this. So again, I put the crystallized rocks on the can, but daddy cautioned me he said "pull slow", I did just that, and this time I got it right. But I didn't feel anything its as if everything was numb, so I began to got scared all over again. Several days went past, and on an alternate basis, we continued testing the waters so to speak. Until it was just as if it was natural or should I say as easy as smoking the weed or snorting the powdered cocaine. Now this is part of our regiment when we would get high and have sex. So I kept my car for a while but this new gift replaced the other. So I had to depend on Dante again.

After 6 months I'd see daddy have a seizure for the first time in my life. I was terrified out of my mind. I called 911, and they came, but he refused to go to the hospital. Later I found out that I inherited them {the seizures} from his side of the family. But nonetheless, daddy had stopped having them. But when he began using this "crack", it triggered something. Dad began going to work less and less. His friends would come over more often than before. One of his friends got fired from the Post Office because of his drug addiction. So he'd be over to our house so often, you'd think he was a resident. This man had gotten so bad his wife kicked him out of the house. So daddy let him stay with us, which to me was not fair. He was taking all of daddy's time. Smoking up all the dope. And I had to cook and clean for him, just like I did for daddy. The good part here is I was not the "wife", I was the "daughter'. Now this to a normal person this would be "good". But to me it was "bad". For one I had to sleep in my own bedroom. I hadn't' done this in almost 3 yrs give or take. That's it, this dude has got to go.

One day I was coming home from school and I spotted a strange car in the carport. Strange because I'd never seen it before in my carport. So I enter the gate, checked it out, then I realized daddy's car is missing. So now I'm curious, as to who's car is this, and where is my daddy's car? So I turn the key to the front door and to my surprise, I see daddy and his friend lounging on the couch laughing and smoking. Usually when I get home I'm greeted with a "hey baby girl", not today. It's as if I didn't even exist. They didn't notice me, I might as well have been invisible. Finally I said "hey dad, I'm home, but nothing. I repeated hey dad I'm home, but they kept on doing what they were doing, as if I didn't exist. So eventually I asked about the car sitting in the carport and the one that was missing from it. The answers blew me away. The car sitting in the carport was daddy's new one. And the other one had been traded. I looked at daddy in astonishment. You see the new car was a Volkswagen bug, and the one he traded was a Lincoln Mark 7, you figure it out. Later that evening I expected daddy to get ready for work, but he didn't, O.K. I thought to myself maybe he took the day off. But this pattern was consistent for 5 says. Finally I asked "daddy you on vacation? He answered yeah permanently". Again I was floored. As for his friend he finally got it together and he went back home. So the cars had to be traded on the count of daddy's job loss, so I thought. But reality its was this, due to his "crack" habit. Daddy traded in the car, for the money.

We've spoken of dramatic life changes and this is only in eight months to a year into this chapter. Another change occurred when I decided I didn't want to be a "wife" anymore. I had Dante, I loved him. Daddy went out of town for the weekend, so I invited Dante over not knowing that daddy had spoken to every neighbor that could view our house. The neighbor in the front, the neighbor on he right, the neighbor on the left. And he asked them to keep an eye on the house not me. I was smart I didn't tell Dante to come over the same night daddy left, but the next night. Besides daddy could've easily doubled back, so I waited to make sure he was gone. By this time I'm 17 1/2, so he trust that I'm able to be alone for the weekend. While at my house Dante, tells me that his mom is sending him to New York to live. What a bomber on this great thing. Yeah I was being selfish. When he told me I got angry and even told him to leave, not hearing the why or when. I was so hurt and mad at the same time. So now what am I going to do? After all I literally made up my mind that I no longer want to sleep with my daddy to be with Dante, and he crush me like this. Devastatingly I accepted it.

Now when daddy returns home, apparently the neighbors had nothing else to do, they reported that there was a young man not only in the the yard but in the house over night, that didn't leave until about 10:00 am the next day. {they had it down to the mark}Each one in agreement with the other. Their reports collaborated so they must be telling the truth. When confronted I at first denied it. But about 3 hours later I approached daddy in a manner like never before. I knocked on the door to the room {something I never did}, daddy said "come in", I slowly pushed the door, nothing happened, he had to remind me "you got to turn the knob". As I entered I said "daddy I need to tell you something, daddy I,". What baby girl? "Daddy, when you was gone I had company". Who? "Dante". Who's that? "My boyfriend". Your what? "My boyfriend". Oh yeah, how long did he stay? "All night?, but, that's not the first time he came over. He come over every night, and has been doing so for about 2 yrs. Now this next conversation will probably make most of y'all's jaws drop in awe but here goes. I told daddy everything about me and Dante. I even said "daddy you got girlfriends, why cant I have a boyfriend"? But then I began to cry, and daddy asked, why are you crying? I replied, "cause he moving to New York." You'd expect daddy to show empathy, or sympathy, but that's not what I got. No, I got disciplined physically, for the first time ever by my daddy. Yeah I got a whoopin. Daddy snatched his belt out his pants and began to lay into me really bad. I had nothing to say, after all this is new. I wailed. I cried. Then I went to my room afterwards and locked my room door. Immediately I began packin my clothes. Remember when the fire gets hot or I don't want to face my wrong doings I run, which is exactly what I was about to do again. Daddy just didn't know what was about to happen. I called my grandma and told her I wanted to come live with her. She said "O.K. Baby".

My 18th birthday was coming up, and I had planned on going out to the club for the first time. The adult club that is, of course I'd been to the teenage clubs, PAC Jam, End Zone, Skating Rink as such. My cousin offered to take me, although I've never spent time with her I said yes. Mind you I do drugs, but I don't drink. So while we're in the club at the bar she ask me what I wanted to drink I say "Hennessy", cause that's what I hear daddy and his friends drink. She said no cuz, you need a lady's drink, so I order a sangria, again she stepped in and interjected her opinion. So finally I said what would you recommend? She says, Long Island iced tea, followed by a blue iced tea, ok I agreed. After all its "only" ice tea, so I thought. I drank them both in bout an hour not realizing the after effects. Yeah I was sooooo green. My cousin then invited me to stay at her house for the night, because we were too far from grandma's house, besides she's family, so its ok right? Now I had been smoking, snorting, and drinking all in the the same night. I felt nauseous, so she said "cuz go get in my bed". Later I awoke to her taking off my clothes, as she stand there stark naked, but I couldn't move or speak. She then proceeded to rape, and molest me. There was nothing I could do, I was too intoxicated. The next day before day could break I was outta there on the first bus to the city from opa-locka smokin. Never to speak to her or at least be alone with her again. Yeah she still family, but you best believe when I saw her I wasn't alone. I'll never get trapped like that ever again. Family, male or female, it doesn't matter. I may have been naive, but not dumb or illiterate. Eventually I told her mom, and she just laughed and said I tried to warn you. Again, just pushing it under the rug. If I'd see her today, I'd tell her I forgive her. Because it taught me to trust nobody but God male or female. Nobody but the Holy Spirit. I VOWED NEVER TO DRINK AGAIN, ONLY ON SPECIAL OCCASIONS AND STILL TO THIS DAY I DON'T DRINK! I still continued to do the familiar weed, cocaine, and crack. You haven't heard me seizing in a while. Because it was so ongoing, that I'd rather mention when they didn't occur. And by this time daddy had lost is house. It was in foreclosure.

One Sunday me and mom went to church, but neither of us was focused on worship really. Our attention was on the clock, we couldn't wait to get home. Because we already had planned to get high, yeah I said it, me and my mom got high together. We both smoked crack cocaine. But this particular Sunday God had other plans. After service we rushed home because we were so anxious to get that "hit". I had some crack at home, and we both decided to be sober and clean going to church so nobody would suspect anything. But of course they knew about her being an addict, but had no clue about my drug use. Man we got in the house, and before we could change our clothes, I picked up the can we used to smoke the crack on, and place a nice sized rock of crack cocaine on it, and as I began to set it ablaze, I heard THE HOLY SPIRIT SAY "NO MORE". Immediately I put the can down. Mom was coming out of the bathroom, and she saw my face, she inquired "what's wrong with you?" "I replied I don't want this anymore. You'd think he say why, or is something wrong with it? She just picked it up and smoked it for herself. I gave her "all" the left over drugs I had stashed away, about $50 worth of crack, $20 worth powdered cocaine, $10 bag of weed. Never to touch it again. Mom was not aware of my encounter with The Holy Spirit. I really didn't understand what happened myself. Eventually mom got into a treatment program and started attending NA meetings, and knowing I also indulged she invited me. So one meeting I did go, and I heard them say something bout a "higher power", and I said to myself I know who my "higher power" is He's the one that stop me from taking my last "hit". So straightaway I concluded I don't need no NA meetings. All I needed was Jesus. You see Jesus had showed me

1. Waisting my money.
2. Your first high is your only high, you'll never get high again.
3. I was killing myself both physically and spiritually.

So there you have it, I quit using just like that no NA meeting, just Jesus, and His covering.

It was a very beautiful afternoon and I was in the family house and the phone rang, I answered, and it was a friend of the family that was incarcerated. So I accepted the call not knowing exactly what that meant. Anyhow, he began to tell me how he was almost about to be released, and he wanted me to do him a favor, O.K. I said. Nothing could prepare me for what he would say next. He said Ive been locked up for so long I just want to be with a lady, so I said O.K. Hypothetically speaking that is, I agreed. We continued to converse for about an hour. Low and behold 2 weeks later I was in the family room watching t.v. and a Society cab pulled up in front of the house. I didn't think nothing of it. The dogs began barking, so I went to the door, apparently this is somebody they are not familiar with, and their's nobody else home. Out stepped this tall dark handsome gentlemen. I took another land and realized it was the family friend I had spoken to on the phone. So I felt comfortable enough to let him in. There was a cold silence in the room for about 10 minutes, finally he said "remember what I asked you over the phone?" Oh my goodness, what had I gotten myself into I thought to myself. I'm now paranoid, but I answer yeah. He say "when we gone do it?" Do what? He said, "you know". So to be true to my word I said soon, trying to put it off as long as I can, because I tell you I'd never believed I would have to fulfill this particular promise. Anyhow I procrastinated for about 3 days, then I had to make due so I regrettably did it. This wasn't easy, I mean, I really didn't know him, had no feelings toward him in that manner, not even sure if he felt some type of way about me. We planned it out. I'd come to his room{he was living there in the family home}. All this sneaking around could cause a ruckus in the family. After all he was much older than me. Besides its really not good because my cousin, who is more like an older brother warned all his friends never to look at any of us as girlfriends. Anyhow after the 2nd time we both became attracted to each other, so now the sneaking around became regular. On a cool Saturday afternoon my aunt said to me "gul/gal, why you looking so big" Auntie what you talking about. You know them old country women know things. She looked at me and flat out said you pregnant. I said no ma'am. She insisted and said yes you is and its Jerry's baby ain't it? Again I denied it. No ma'am auntie, why don't i just give her the right answer, the truth. She then calls Jerry into her room, and questioned him. You see I couldn't hold water I'd always tell on myself. Anyway this discovery happened when I was 3 months pregnant. So now I had to move in with him in his room. He was responsible for me now. That's just how it had to be. Again I haven't mentioned any seizure activity. I stopped having them, Thank God. Now Jerry was lucky that everybody was okay with us being together, because it could've ended badly. This was during the time of great thunder storms in 1993, I was about 8 3/4 months ready and due to deliver. I had a craving for Burger King, so Jerry went out in the raining storm crossed I-95 freeway, to get me a bacon double cheese burger, but Burger King was closed weather. Yeah he risked his life so that Icould have what I wanted. That's usually how I operated, "I'm gone get what I want when I want it", God made me special. Then on February 6, we were having (relations) regularly because the doctor said it would speed up the labor, I was overdue. Then on February 7, I started having contractions, they took me to the hospital. It was decided to induce my labor due to me be epileptic, mom went to McDonalds to get something to eat and when she returned, I'd had a baby girl. Yep, Tredella was born, thus ending this chapter and leading up to the next one, where now I'm embracing life. No drugs, no seizures, enjoying being a parent.

5

EMBRACING LIFE

Intro
This new life as a parent is both good and bad for me. Thank God I have plenty of help. I got my mom, grandma, auntie, sisters, and brother, yeah my siblings are younger than me but they too has been a helping hand. One day I heard them arguing about who gonna get the baby while I rested.

Most of my post natural activity was sleep, sleep, and more sleep. I tried to breastfeed Tredella but she refused, thank God for that, because I've heard that its painful, and I didn't want to endure any more pain at this time. Giving birth and post birth is enough. Nothing was on my mind but Tredella at this time. What she was gonna wear. I made certain that she had the best. Being the best mom I could. Spending all my money on my baby. She had expensive shoes, name brand clothes, and she couldn't even walk, she wasn't even wearing

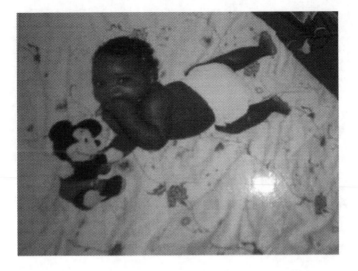

clothes she still was in onesies. Her daddy was so elated about the fact that he had a girl that sometimes I'd catch him crying in secret. So for the first 2yrs of Tredella's life all was well. We even moved into our own place, mind you it was adjacent to another apartment which was my mom's and my siblings occupied, and they'd come over to get Tredella so often you'd think they gave birth to her. But I needed the break. I mean "Barney The Dinosaur" is good sometimes, but for my baby it was "all" my baby wanted. So I didn't mind them coming to rescue me.

One night very late, early morning me and Jerry go get in the bed together. It's my house so I don't have to worry about no one coming in, so I often times slept in the buff. But this particular night, I went to sleep right away. And I turned over later that night and I didn't feel Jerry but I saw the T.V. In the living room flashing so I figured he went into the living room to watch T.V. (His favorite type of movies), so I drifted on back to sleep. I couldn't rest peacefully so again I reached for him, he's still not in the bed, tv still flashing, maybe he fell asleep out there. But to my surprise he's not on the couch so I call his name Jerry, and as I'm walking through the house, I catch him running out of Tredella's room with his genitals erect, and he barges past me to get to the bathroom. So I asked, what's wrong? What's going here? And he answered, "what ever you think is happening is happening". So he immediately confessed to molesting our daughter. I in suspense now say to him "what you said?, he replied with the same answer. So I rushed to Tredella's room and she sitting up in her bed, asking for her daddy. Remembering my childhood I instantaneously reacted, I grabbed Tredella and took her next door to my mom's house, and told them what I had witnessed, But they didn't believe me. So angrily I rush back to my apartment and call the police, but meanwhile Jerry has shut himself up in the bathroom. As I'm looking for my shoes, I come across a mirror with powdered cocaine on it. So right there I put 2 and 2 together, and I get even more angry, knowing this is how it began with me, and this could've been a repeat performance going on in my home, I didn't know.

So. I call Ma, and tell her what happened, and she tells me to get out of the house, because now I am extremely furious with Jerry. No telling what I might do. So I start off walking toward Ma's house, mind you, I was in the buff. So I just pulled on some pants and t-shirt, since I was going just next door. So here I am walking down the street in my t-shirt, no bra, and pull on pants. Everybody can see something was up, because I'm walking like I have to get somewhere fast. Focusing only on the place I have to get to. In the middle of the road, no I'm not worried about no cars or whatever. I need to get to the only one that can calm me down, and that's my Ma. She can calm an angry buffalo from charging at another during mating season. She was just that sweet, and her spirit (aura) always gentle. By the time I reached her home which was about 5 city blocks from mine, I had people walking with me as if we were going to war. But everyone knew I'd never done anything out of sync, but this was a different Tanya, they never seen this character before. Because I tell you, the only thing on my mind at this time was murder or castration. Yeah I, The One Who's always calm, nonchalant, and quiet. Was at this time loud and boisterous not in my words or voice, but through my attitude an actions. When I reached Ma's house and told her what happened, she just put me in her arms and I just sobbed, like never before. "Ma said "dats right baby get all out". The police came to Ma's house, because in my anxiety, agitation, and trepidation, I gave them Ma's address instead of mine? God did it. They questioned me and I told them everything, I mean come on now, how could a grown man that has a a whole woman, lying in the bed with him stark naked and willing to please him, direct his sexual tendencies on 2yr old baby girl. This was very hard for me, because I too went through molestation and incest. So that just caused my anger to turn to fury. But Thank God for Ma. So I get in the car with police and go back to my house and low and behold, he (Jerry) is sitting in the living room waiting for the police to come take him away. It's almost like he wanted to be caught a locked back up like a caged animal. At this point I'm baffled.

One week goes by, one month, 2 months, and I'm still angry. I see something about Job Corps in the welfare office, I inquire about it and I made up my mind, "this is what I'm gonna do, its may way out". Besides, Tredella's with my mom now anyhow. Oh, and for those that are curious and concerned about Tredella's well being, she was not penetrated, Thank God. God blocked it, He wouldn't let it be so. Oh Jesus you are the center of my joy. So the day comes when I am leaving to go to Albany, Georgia. Supposedly for 2yrs, oh but God. I ain't ashamed to say while there I was faced with a sexual identity situation time and time again. All that reflected back in my memory was of my cousin taking advantage of me on my 18 birthday, what a gift. No not. Here I'm faced with the same situation, and it seemed like all the girls in my dorm was with it, but a few was against it. "Let me put clause in here, I'm not homophobic, I respect another person's choices, but for me I pass." So I got with one of the Professors and explained to her how I wanted to leave. She asked why, "you're doing so well, you only got a half way through, and at the rate you're going you might get there faster." So I came up with a cover-up, I miss my baby. She explained if I changed my major, then some of the classes I've already completed goes toward that and it gets me closer to the end. So I did, I changed from administrative, to creative writing. I was outta there in 9 months, they changed my floor not dorm. Tell me God doesn't go before us and I have to disagree. He goes ahead of us, and dispatches angels to make the rough ways smoothe, and the crooked ways straight.

Now y'all may be wandering about Jerry, well like I say he was waiting for the police, because he knew he was guilty. So they arrested him and he was in prison for some time. Now I'm back in Miami, finished my tenure at Job Corps. Now I just wanna work have my own. Not being dependent on nobody. So I'd always said I wanna be a police officer, so I decided to start slow. So I arranged it where I'd be taking classes in business education in the fall of 1996 at Miami Dade Community College and I continued in that class until April of 1997. Remember I love criminal justice, so I decided to take the class for armed security officer. All was going well. Tredella is still with my mom, and I'm just living with grandma. I passed the tests and was issued a permit to carry, and a job. God did it. You'd think they not supposed to give me a permit because of the seizures, mind you, I really haven't had as many as before. And when I was pregnant I didn't have any. But then I applied for the Police academy and they denied me, not 1 time but 3 times. I was persistent like the woman and the unjust judge. So I took another avenue.

Remember I always had the best, but I had to work for it. I wasn't about no handouts of any kind, but everybody kept reminding me that I had a seizure disorder, so I shouldn't be working. But I chose to do the opposite by becoming an Insurance Agent. One scorching hot day, I had an appointment with a lady at 1:30pm far from where I lived. And at that time I didn't have a car, so I had to catch two buses, and walk almost half a mile to get to this lady's house. So of course I was late, but to my surprise my manager had already gotten to the appointment and she sold the woman the policy on her on behalf and she received the credit. I wont get no perks for this sale, not even as in recognition of me being the agent. So now I'm upset, confused, and wouldn't you know it, I had a seizure in the woman's house. They call the ambulance, and I'm hospitalized for 2 days. I immediately vowed I will no longer participate in anything having to do with an insurance company, at least not that one.

Daddy is now living in another home. I'd visit him from time to time. And neither of us bring up our past, as far as we are concerned it never happened. Now my solid rock my "Ma" (grandma) is transitioned from earth to Heaven, I'm truly crushed. For one my family chooses to not tell me right away, due to our closeness and my sickness. They were looking out for me. Oh, how this crushed me. I couldn't fathom the thought of her being gone. The day of the funeral comes and everybody is surrounding me, asking me if I was ok, yes I replied constantly. Until when we got to the cemetery, that's when I lost it, and my friend Selena (whom I met and became close friends with at Miami Dade Community College) had to comfort me. The Bible says "you could be entertaining an angel and not be aware" (Hebrews 13:2 NIV). And at that time she was my angel.

I called this embracing life, because now I'm living every women's dream. I'm married now, yeah my husband was at "Ma's" home going, but there was nothing he could do. So here I am embracing the love of being married. I feel like a queen and I have a king that has been granted permission to take care of me, and he did just that.

Do many understand that even the devil knows your desires. So I loved this man, not even realizing he didn't feel the same about me. I was so naive. (Green as we called it). Because the only men I ever loved hurt me, and yet I still loved them. One very humid Sunday afternoon while riding on the church bus, I ask the driver to stop by my husband's house. Yes, you heard right. I was just that gullible, that I agreed to allow him to live in his own house, while I stayed with family. It's as I was a wife waiting for a husband to return from deployment. To clear your curiosity, yes were legally married. So we pull up to his house and I ranged the doorbell, no answer. Knock no answer, but as I peered through a window I get a glimpse of something or someone moving. I decided to go around the side of the house and take a second look and to my surprise or maybe y'all might be saying my ignorance, he was with another woman. We never consummated our marriage. We dated for a whole year and still never had any intimate relations. But you see God was setting me up because even here all I did was politely return to the bus and say, he was asleep. Sometimes embracing it is accepting it. So I accepted that he wasn't for me. Should I be angry and enraged, yes and rightfully so. But the God I serve reminded me vengeance is mine. And that he was working everything together for my good. Now I didn't completely understand that then, but I grasped what I could and I held on to it. So I got out, it wasn't real anyhow.

My transparency will be your mirror image. And by glancing in you'll catch the flaws before they get out of hand. To embrace also causes you to sometimes become enthusiastic or passionate. Well at this point my view was looking out for those that don't have. Then I too became one of those. You see after the incident with my husband I no longer was being funded by him, so people began to act funny. Because my heart was generous, if you asked and I had it so did you, even if it was my last. Yeah I saw you were trying to bamboozle me, but I didn't care. I knew God would provide.

By now my baby girl and me one day after school arrive home and no one is there to greet us. The house was practically empty. They did leave some food in the fridge. Evening came, no one showed up. Next morning still no one but me and my baby. Like usual I ran errands throughout the day, picked up my baby from school and again we go to an empty home. Maybe their away for a few days I thought, it is spring time. I go to give my baby a bath and nothing comes out of the tap. Now I'm no plumber nor handyman but I tried everything I knew or seen done, still zilch, dry as a desert. O.k. My awareness antennas are going up. I heard, or should

I say I was warned about the shadiness of this character. Still I ignored them. Come on this is family I thought to myself, not remembering they'll be the first to stab you in the back if their hearts aren't right. Well she goes to church, she shouts all day long "Hallelujah this, Praise God that". I didn't know about testing spirits to see if they are of or from God. I didn't know anything about being weary of pretenders, or truly understand what hypocrisy was then. So I embraced every branch she extended. But the final straw was this, and I give God the total Glory for this one, not only had we no lights but no water either and we lived there 2wks. Going to neighbors and asking them for buckets of water, staying out while its day, and using candles at night, imagine that, But God.

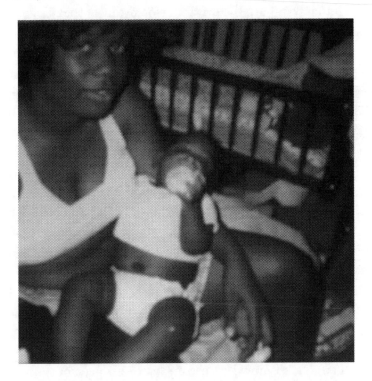

This goes even deeper I'd seen an ad for a room for rent, so I answered it, and our struggles were over, so I thought. We packed what little we had and moved in, this was certainly better living conditions right? You'd think so, at least we got water and lights. That's why when I see people that live in other countries where these things are not available I cant do nothing but Thank God. At our new place of residence the land lady was very abhorrent. But I had to endure this for my baby, I knew God didn't bring me this far to leave me. Not understanding that he was in "full control". Uh oh somebody at "Della's school found out about our previous living conditions, and called Homeless Hotline not CPS, only God. But before they could help us, the land lady changed locations and invited us to come.

We talking about embracing right, so that's just what I did, I embraced the opportunity, if not we'd truly be homeless. Within 3wks in our new location I got a call, oh God, I tell you the joy that I felt when the man on the line described who he was. He said to me "Ms. Clesidor-Smith, I'll be there to pick you up in about 3hrs, to take you to a shelter". Though I'd never been in one before, I was ecstatic and replied yes sir. Della and the land lady's daughter had now developed a friendship more like sisters, so I regretted having to tell her, again were moving, but I did. And telling Ms. Ma'am was no balloon party either. Around 7:30pm a man arrived wearing a green t-shirt and knocked on the door. I'd been standing on the balcony for about an hour anyhow, when I spotted this strange government looking car pull up. Fearing the process, I went inside. I'd heard of some strange things occurring in shelters, again I was enthusiastically happy and over joyed when he asked for me. Embracing this change taught me that Gods ways is not always our ways, and Gods timing is never our timing. We arrived at this place that was so secluded, fear began to overwhelm me, but anxiety was the greater feeling. We were assigned a room, and even then, immediately when I entered the room an indescribable peace came over me, along with empathy for the other mother's that were there. It was about 11pm, so we didn't want to disturb anybody especially the babies, so we went to sleep. The next day I was awaken by one of the mothers telling me about breakfast. Now "Red" was one that seemed angry but was very peaceful and peaceable, she just fell on "hard times". She had been there for about 8 months already and about to be placed in her own apartment. God did it. Most of the time here I'd just stay in my room, and Della would be in the daycare. But she was missing our family, and if anyone knows while in shelters you usually cant disclose your location, and most of all you have to follow strict rules, which include curfews. But God had a different plan. I embraced this part of my life not as a let down, but as a slow down. God did some wonderful things. He fixed it that Della could not only visit the family, but spend the night with them as well. We didn't have to eat the shelter's food, which at first I was grateful for. But one morning Della was eating breakfast in the chow hall, and she got sick. So I'd use my Food Stamps to buy us something, and go to friends house to cook it. Finally, God made it where we had extra money to eat out. Jesus is a way maker. Yeah these people had began embracing us like family.

Now after we'd been there for about 9 months, it was time for my review, and my counselor remembered I'd told her about my security license, and God did the rest. She called me in, sent me on an interview, I got the job, and was set up for my own place within 1 wk. But I'm still human. And I was smoking cigarettes, and attending church. This "dude" sees me after I had gotten hired on the spot on the way to the bus stop. In my arrogance, I lit a cigarette and I here "psst, psst, hey black you got one for me"? Me being me, goes in my purse and give him one. Then he stirs up a conversation. Coming from work? No, I replied, ok, you go to the Job Corp, he asked? No, I replied again, and before he could say anything else I said "I'm pregnant". He looked at me up and down, you don't look pregnant. Then I hit him with it, "that's because I'm pregnant in the Holy Ghost", this was to let him know the kind of woman he was dealing with. Besides God was blessing me so much, I had no time for no man. "Just give me your number, maybe I'll go to church with you on Sunday". So of course I obliged him, and I was on my way. When I got back to the shelter "Red" was packing her things and the other lady in the room was at work. She was the one that let my counselor know of the opening at her job, besides we were like sisters. Remember I said "the people here were embracing me like family". My sister and I would go to work together and come home together. Our kids were in the same school, the shelter was associated with. We both decided to work extra hard to amp our chances of getting our own places. I mean all we need was a "portion" of the money and the connected charities would take it from there. God was working on my behalf even when it seemed like it was not possible. Oh yeah the "dude" never knew about the shelter. By the time I spoke to him again, I was in my own place. Rent paid for 1 whole year, utilities paid for 1 year, furniture and everything taken care of. "Yeah I'm Embracing this. Which may have been a little more than I had bargained for or was it?

6

MINE EYES HAS SEEN THE GLORY

Intro

So lets understand this whole mine eyes thing. I'm speaking of both my spiritual and carnal eyes. They both a being opened. I realize now that God is doing remarkable things, not just for me, but for me to Glorify Him. So yeah i now began to proclaim and announce to others "The Glory of God". But my carnal eyes see some things I'm attracted to as well. God was telling me or should i say warning me to "come out from amongst them and be ye separate". But my carnal eyes and needs over rid that.

After I had barely settled in my new apartment as I said, the young man I met while in the shelter (Warren) called, and asked to go to church the next time I go. Blindly I said ok. Sunday came, and he went to church with me and he seemed ok, so I invited him over for a home cooked dinner for a first date. Listen my Spiritual eyes was focusing on the presence of The Glory of God, but my carnal eyes was focusing on my flesh. Let's be real. I hadn't been with a man for over a year and a half. But i wasn't "thirsty". Nonetheless I am human. I never asked him if he was seeing someone else. I wasn't trying to go that deep. The day of the date came, and I prepared a delicious spaghetti and garlic bread dinner. With a side of kool aid, yeah the red kind. We ate dinner, Della went to her room. They had bonded within the 2 days. She said mommy I like him. I don't know what she was thinking, but I said "he ok as a friend". So I go to clean the kitchen and he come pressing up on me, oh my goodness, he don't know what he doing, so I say NO firmly!! That's not what I'm about. He insisted, this time trying to remove my clothes, I screamed, pushed him away and ran into my room. Now listen my daughter knew something was up. Because I got my car keys and I ran to the car. But thank God I didn't come back up. I just called my dad and told him I was bringing my gun to him, I didn't need around me. You see I had began to be awakened to the truth. Do not be easily provoked in your Spirit, for anger resides in the laps of fools. My Spiritual eyes saw "The Glory", and said "why would I give all this up for him", plus lose my daughter? So I politely went back upstairs after about 2 hours, (giving myself enough time to calm down) and asked him to leave. I didn't want to have nothing to do with him again. Of course, he realized his actions and apologized, but that wasn't good enough for me. The devil was trying to distract what God had planned for me. Because like I said I began to see "The Glory of The God.

"The Glory is the presence of The Lord. Where the presence of The Lord is there is liberty. Liberty to Praise Him, so now "my praise is different". I had spoken of being pregnant in The Holy Ghost not fully understanding what that meant. But it was absolutely true. I was going through the different trimesters of spiritual pregnancy. First trimester is, becoming aware and realizing that you are carrying something precious. Second trimester, protecting, feeding, and keeping yourself as the carrier/surrogate out of situations that could cause you to abort the baby or have a premature baby. And the third trimester is, surrounding yourself with midwives that can help you through your birthing process. But just remember just like in the book of Revelations "the dragon" didn't want the woman to give birth to baby boy, he was right there waiting to kill it, he's was doing the same thing because I was carrying a "spiritual baby" at that time. HALLELUJAH GOD WE PRAISE YOU, HELP US TO SEE YOUR GLORY!!!

So now I'm doing what I can to protect "my spiritual baby". I get a call from Warren, I don't to talk to him, so I ignore his call. The devil knows our "every" weakness. And we as babes in Christ can't detect the tactics of the enemy. So he called again. Besides I am just realizing that God "called" me, and walking cautiously into my "vocation, office, and calling" yet my carnal self is still present so I give in. I invite him to church, he comes over, and guess what I have a seizure. Now anything can happen. I don't really know this man. He could rape me, rob me, anything. But what did he do. He took care of me. Made sure I was ok. And insisted on staying overnight. Sleeping on the couch, whilst I slept in the bedroom. Which now cause me to change my thoughts and vision of him. Usually it takes 3-5 days to recover from a seizure and he was there all the time, making sure I ate and everything. So yes I'm falling for him. I mean he knows I have seizures and he didn't run, that right there is a check on my checklist. Another Sunday came around and we go to church and the "message" the Pastor gave was a powerhouse. We couldn't stop discussing it. "The word of God convicts us and brings us to a place of repentance". And though he tried to, the devil couldn't be in my presence and continue to deceive me. Gods word is alive and active. It's sharper than any double edged sword piercing soul and spirit, bone and marrow. It was that word that caused Warren to speak these words "Tanya I got to tell you something." What I asked, because the word goes on to say "nothing is hidden from God. He sees everything, even the thoughts and the intents of the heart. The Glory of The Lord, His presence caused Warren, to disclose to me that he had an encounter his ex, while he was courting me. His excuse was I sent him home, so he had no other choice, after all he is a man with needs. At that very moment I realized that this was happening for a reason so I didn't fight it. I'd been studying the Bible, and allowing it to continue to change me as in Romans 12:2. I was no longer comfortable with worldly things. I mean I was never one to really hangout, clubbing was never my forte. I'm no longer doing drugs. I'm at a point in my life where I'm seeking God and His purpose for me. And in doing so I came across this scripture 2 Timothy 2:15 and it stuck with me. So I forgave him and we continued to grow closer and his bond with Della was great.

One day I said I need to paint my apartment he volunteered for that. Della wanted a fish tank He paid for that. Now I'm feeling him out again. Yes I'm still working. But I have nothing to pay. So now my tithes is more than the regular 10%, plus I'm giving to different charities. My carnal self said I got more than 10% so I'll give you 40%. I wasn't worried about what was being done with or about the money. I just was doing it to please people. Showing off!!

Warren asked to move in. He's now staying extended weekends. Taking care of Tredella, cooking, cleaning, ironing my uniforms, all that good stuff. So I say "let me think about it". Why isn't he working you may ask? I did, he was in the process of getting his CDL license, so I waited. But I was not paying attention. I'll explain that later. I see The Glory, someone to take care of the house, and my daughter whilst I work, because I loved my job. I'd work long hours, because I loved it just that much. This is where I was spreading The Gospel, teaching the young folks about Jesus. They'd just flock to me to share their problems, concerns, situations. It was almost like I was a counselor instead of a security officer and yes, I love it. About 9 months on the job I had a seizure and it through up a red flag. They put me on leave for about 3 wks. And while I was home Warren got his license, but nobody was hiring at that time. So now I'm at the halfway point of my payment mark, so all is well. But I've always had an expensive taste. Yes, thank my daddy for that. Speaking of daddy, he is now living in an apartment (assistant living facility) and is too in the church. He's established a relationship with Christ. I had to be sure of this, before I took Warren to meet him. You know over protective father syndrome, well with our history; lets just say it could of gone a totally different way, the outcome. I rather not even think of it. So I take Warren to meet daddy. And the normal grill and drill of what do you do for living, came up, Warren replied, I'm a truck driver sir, and that quickly sealed the deal. That's daddy's career as well, but now he's retired.

So now my carnal eyes begin to see different things. Let's jump to the next 4 months after I've returned back to work. Warren is living with me doing construction work, instead of driving trucks. Tredella spending a lot time with my mom. One Spring evening on my way home from work I felt weird. My heart began to fluster, I seemed as if I was in 3 dimensional movie. I was overcome with fear, because I know what this is. But I'm driving, what should I do? Pull over and try to get someone's attention? How? I don't know what happened, before I could gather my thoughts, I hear, ma'am are you ok. I'm trying to figure out who, what, where, why? Then I realized oh my I had a seizure while I was driving. But that's not the only part to give "God The Glory" for. They tell me the that the car flipped over and landed in a ditch on the side of State Road 826, but yet I'm still alive, Glory to God. He Kept me. So of course I was out of work for about 9wks. I'm not lazy when it comes to work, especially if it is something I enjoy doing. By this time I had established personal relationships with my students.

Remember I said "I wasn't paying attention". Warren would call the job every hour. Sometimes when he dropped me off for work, because now I'm no longer driving myself to work, he'd stay around. Sneaking on campus, watching everything I was doing. Questioning my co-workers, especially about their relationships with me. Even the male students, he was jealous of how close I was with them. Now one of my students was "slinging" and Warren found out about it, and asked me to make a deal for a large exchange on behalf of somebody else. Never did he imply he was investing in this deal. So it took about 3 weeks, yeah I had that much "juice" influence. So now the day come and we get ready to make the exchange and Warren just flip out on me. I mean, duh, I got to isolate me and the young man in order for the deal to happen, but Warren totally aborted the plan. He charged into the office yelling and screaming innuendos about me and the young man which were further from the truth. All of this is occurring in the front of the school so the officers are trying to get order. I go to the back of the office and Warren chases me out the back door and chokes me. It literally took 2 of the male officers to get him off of me. And I'm looking like a fool, you told me to do this. I was trying to help you and your friends. I couldn't see the insecurity in the beginning, but as time went on he revealed it. So now here I am probably facing termination. Because I will not jeopardize the young man's future and disclose what was truly happening so we lied and said it was a domestic dispute gone wild. We left out the student. So when I was questioned by the staff leader, that was what everybody agreed to. Even as officers, our loyalty to is we'll stick by each other's side no matter what, and that's just what happened. Thank God for true Loyalty. Yes, I got fired, but due to sickness and not to foolishness. You see, it was decided by my Chief that my sickness was jeopardizing my ability to work. Letting me go was the best option, at least this way I can still collect disability, or social security, or unemployment, without penalty. My eyes has seen the glory. Say Favor. My family did not appreciate the fact that Warren put his hands on me. They decided that they were going to "lay hands on him", not spiritual hands either. But by that time, yeah myself forgave him yet again. So we went to visit mom for a cookout, and they had it planned. I told Warren to stay in the car, because I knew how overprotective everybody is over me. I don't do nothing to anybody. I'm different than the rest. There are some special qualities and characteristics in me that others don't have, just for that alone I stand out. So I say to Warren," let me go talk to them first. Try to smooth things over. Really the damage is already done. And all these people care. they were angry, because it was me. Again say Favor. So I told my mom that all was well between Warren and I. Then I proceeded upstairs to tell my brother the same thing, to "call off the dogs" so to speak, and it seemed good to me. But I didn't know the lingo of street. And they was talking amongst themselves my brother and his friends. I go to get Warren so he could apologize. And we walked in the house and immediately the atmosphere was cold, you knew something was shifty but couldn't tell exactly what? Those boys jumped on Warren like a hyena on a gazelle. I tried to intervene but I was shoved into another room. They pummeled him for at least 15 minutes, while I was in the other room screaming, "please, stop, its ok, I love him"", all kinds of things, to try to get them to leave him alone. Finally, I guess they got tired, I grabbed Warren and we got in the car and bolted out of there. He called "his people", and come to find out "his people", were our family members, they all grew up together. And when they found out what had happened they too were shocked that he laid hands on me. Come on Jesus. My eyes have seen the glory. I don't visit mom for a while.

Meanwhile, I'm no longer working. Warren is working off and on, its time now for the rent to be paid the year is up. Look at God, just when the provisions are gone, my job is taken away. Now you may be saying that's the devil, no actually its God showing up. Cause while all this going on, after I receiving unemployment, my disability will begin. Yet this Spiritual baby is kicking, so now I now become a student like Timothy in the Bible, not only listening and hearing what the pastor is saying, but I got to study for myself to get the full knowledge and wisdom of it. Warren now lands a permanent job, and I find out that the rent is only half the full amount for the months. I tell you, trusting God is a process, and sometimes we don't understand why He does the things He does, but He knows. So now what could I do now but get into The Word. I'm not working. So now after I clean up, I'm studying something in The Bible. I think this is where I realized God had just began to push me into ministry. So I needed to be in an environment appropriate for this. But remember satan is waiting for this baby too. He wants to kill it immediately, so if he can get you to abort it, or give birth prematurely he will by any means necessary. So now Warren is working. But he's acting a little peculiar. He's being funny about his ways. He's not himself. What is this? My carnal eyes detected it. He using some type of drug. Remember I used them. I grew up in this environment. So now I'm watching out for tel-tell signs. He doing normal things, hanging out with the neighbor downstairs, ok, nothing wrong with that. So now time come to pay the bills and this month we short, ok I fill in with my side money. Yeah I got my own money, my "Ma always told me keep yo own money on the side just in case". He's working less days, waking up later than usual, wait a minute, what's really happening? So I ask him, and he says to me, "I got to go to the store". You've been hangin around that store too much, and in my curiosity I inquire with the neighbors and find out that its a trap house (drug hole). Later that evening, as he's watching tv, I interrupt asking calmly, so this what you doing with your money. But I realize I'm speaking these words to myself. It's a rehearsal of what I'm going to do. I'm not good with confrontation. So weeks go by before I even think of addressing the situation. My eyes has seen the glory.

We get a new next door neighbor, and he and Warren were inseparable, like Cheech and Chong or Kid and Play. When you saw one you saw the other. Anyhow one day Warren wakes up to go to work early in the morning and by 10am he's back, I asked him why you home so early? He said, "the job gave some of us a few days off. Ok, But now he's over to the neighbors house more than home. Oh yeah, I found out at the store was one of his old friends he grew up with, and he was the head dealer. So Warren was crediting his drugs. Promising to pay whenever he got payed. But when he couldn't, he would use the money for the utilities instead. I really didn't know that was going on. But I just couldn't shake this dude. Here we are 2 and1/2 yrs, and I'm still with him despite everything I know about him. Then I realized I was trying to give him the opportunity to change so I let it slide. Yeah you probably saying where is the glory in that? Well, I kept my apartment, my car, my sanity, and I didn't fall back. I know they say once an addict always an addict, I beg to differ. Once Jesus delivered me from drugs I never went back, and never will. But yes I'm still smoking cigarettes, going to church, but see I didn't realize that God's plan was working. I even began to judge myself and feel guilty causing me to stop going to church for over 4 months, but still then God was working it all together for my good.

We've now been in the apartment 3 yrs, and my disability is covering the utilities and such. Warren is responsible for the rent. So when the rent man spoke to me about the rent being late, I was taken a back. So I questioned Warren, his excuse was "the man made a mistake". So the next month the landlord came knocking saying the rent was late again, which now puts us 2 months in arrears, I said "I'll take care of it, give me 2 wks. So I go to "my secret stash", and this nigga done stole my money. I go to check my purse the same thing. I'm supposed to dump this square right here, this moment. But I know the blessing on my life, so now I try to change him. Yeah, I became "Captain save a bro". Third month roll around and we have to leave, all this time everything was going well, now I'm getting evicted. I know the characteristics of an addict, these are the things that go with using, especially loss of budgeting finances, so I just roll with it. But yes my eyes have seen the glory, you see, I'm not focused on the right now, I'm looking for the far ahead, and it gives me peace. We move in with his mother. Yeah, he's a "momma's boy". She think her son can do no wrong. But when I disclose to her what happened, she said oh no, he didn't start that again. So wait a minute you telling me he did this before. Why nobody told me? That's when God began to speak to me, and say "try the spirit by the spirit to see if its from God. Now this sounds easy, but remember I'm now probably a 3rd grader in the spiritual realm. But yes I'm pregnant, and all I need is the right timing or should I say God's timing and the birth will occur. So were there for about 2wks and I wouldn't have relations with him in his momma's house. Gross, disrespectful to his momma and me. He get mad. Now got an attitude with me, and his momma don't have the faintest idea why. She now sees something different in me. She recognizes that I am a child of God. So asks me to attend her church, but remember I'm a faithful member of my own church. I'm now a Deaconess, Sunday School Teacher, Powerful Influence, helping in all areas of the church.......besides my whole family grew up in this church, its a legacy. But I noticed that something was happening, God was taking me in a different direction. So I took her up on her invitation. I'd hear her talking about speaking in tongues, we'd never do that at my church. Shouting, giving God Praise in Radical way was prohibited at my church. It was too conservative. The most we could do is wave our hands, and not too high or too long. The usher, would do just that, usher you out into the vestibule, or bathroom, until you gather yourself together. Well, while we were at his mom's house eating dinner one of the sisters from the church came to visit, and Warren walked in the room, she whispered to the sister "he fighting with that addiction demon again". The sister told her to bring him to church, so he can tarry until he is truly delivered. Ive never heard any of this stuff before. All I know is God is The Father, Jesus is our Savior, Love your neighbor, you know the basics. I tell you I knew more about about raising money for church events and how to work in the kitchen. So I knew the works of a servant. Which I enjoyed. I enjoyed being hospitable to the people. But I didn't realize God was preparing me for my next stage in life. Jeremiah 29: 11, tells us That God knows the plan He has for us.

After 7 months living with his mom she tells us about a cousin she has that is willing to allow us to live in her house rent free. All we have to do is pay the utilities. My eyes have seen the glory, say it with me "favor". So we move in the next week. Yes, his momma furnished the placed, because we lost everything I'd acquired before. Dishes, sheets, appliances, furniture, even clothes. This time it all came from her. By this time Tredella is now living with my mom, I didn't want to take her away from the family again. Besides she's at the age where she can understand, and she is highly upset with him. As a matter of fact their relationship is estranged. But I still cant shake him. I mean usually by this time I would have cut him lose long time ago. But for some reason I cant get rid of him. My eyes have seen the glory. I realize God is truly up to something. Warren even seemed to have stopped using. Well of course he couldn't do it in his momma's house. So now this is the Warren I knew before loving, kind, caring, taking care of what needs to be done. But then something happened. He begin to question my every move, my doctor's appointments, when I went to the store, when I went to church, any move I made he questioned. This made me suspicious. He began to accuse me of stepping out on him. Boy please, I don't get down like that. Besides I got you. I'm afraid of the repercussions of cheating, you know diseases. Don't you think I respect you and honor you more than that? Or maybe you forgot I am a woman of God and regard myself in this manner. I respect me and I fear God. So this happened continuously, but he never questioned my money. You see I'm not proud of it, but I used my sickness to get paid. And to make it ok, I'd tell myself, God is not finished with me yet. I was still doing things that wasn't right. Wait are you judging Warren for his addiction, but you are illegally getting money, you hypocrite. Mine eyes have seen the glory, yes, So I stop doing that.

My daughter said to me on her 16th birthday, she wanted a party. My baby got to have the best, so I asked her what was her menu, I tried To accommodate her. I asked about music and other things, I was trying to make up for the time I was out of her life. I have to admit I was acting out of guilt. So the amount of money was not a factor. I had planned a surprise she'd never forget. So while we were in the kitchen preparing the food, somebody said "yo there's a strange car pulling up", nobody recognized the car. So when he stepped out we were all shocked. The he I'm speaking of is Tredella's dad, he had been released and in contact with my mom, for a while. So they invited him to the party. Tredella was so happy to see him, he handed her a letter he wrote her in prison and she was relieved and forgave him. My eyes has seen the glory. My carnal eyes stepped in and said now they will see and know, as in the tone of vengeance and malice. But I was reminded a that moment, let God handle it. Vengeance is mine saith The Lord. Just imagine the pain I felt when he walked in and they received him without question. I went back mentally to the day of my child's departure from her father. But I calmly said yes Lord. You see God was always in the presence that's why its called, I have seen the glory.

Following this Tredella would come to my house often but she still had reservations about Warren. And one evening while the tv was on divorce court, Tredella got belligerent, she wanted to watch something else. I said to her, Tredella I don't care if you're mad with him, I taught you respect. And she spoke something like you on his side now under her breath, before I knew it I had jacked Tredella up by the throat, and she had the audacity to pull a knife on me. So I called the police, for both her sake and mine. But I'd never press any charges against her. It was meant to teach her a lesson. Actually all this was distracting me from what was really happening I was seeing the vision of my ministry. In bits and pieces. Several months later Della went Job Corps in Jacksonville, so that was that. God began to speak to me about Habakkuk, write the vision and make it plain. So I began putting the pieces together. My ministry, the purpose for it. For whom it was for. But still it was a little fuzzy, but at last I got that much out of it. Now my Spiritual Pregnancy is now evolving into the second trimester. I've now graduated into grade 8 in the spiritual realm, so I haven't even gotten to high school yet. So the enemy detected this before I did, he feels he can still over power me. Because I tell you the truth at times I was double minded, wasn't absolutely sure. One minute I'm all in, then something happens and my fears cause me to question my calling. But the Bible declares that we should count it all joy, when we face trials. My Eyes are seeing the Glory. God test our faith, to show our maturity and wisdom. But in junior high you don't have the level of maturity you need. But Jesus already prayed that my faith not to fail, "it is written". We lived with his mom's cousin for about 4yrs. Then she makes arrangements for us to live in another rent free home. And I'm questioning why is she doing this now? I didn't know her cousin was too sickly to stay in her home any longer. I'd go over to Auntie's (I called her Auntie) house and sit with her, pray with her, and just talk and listen. If she needed me to go to the store I'd go. Maybe I'd cook for her, Whatever. But then out of blue, somebody comes up and now they want to put her in a home and take over the property. Where were they before? Which means we either have to start paying rent, which I was already giving Auntie a stipend. Come on now y'all know rent free ain't rent free. I believed she did deserve something, that's how I was raised. The last choice we had is move. So that's what we chose. So this knew place belonged to one of his mother's friends that passed within the pass month. She was his care taker, he had no kids, so now, she say, "all y'all have to do is pay the the taxes, and utilities.

Again I'm not all the way in. I'm still smoking cigarettes, and I've even went back to making money illegally. But yet God Glory is on my life. Hallelujah, he's just waiting for me. My eyes see the the glory. You see the house we moved in now is surrounded by churches. One on the left and one in the the back, one on the corner, and one right down the street. I cant get away from this calling. So now I attend one of Warren's mom church services and "wow". I'd never been moved like that before. Even in my church, I'd feel a little different but not like this. You see in my church you couldn't shout, or even wave your hands. They'd shush you. But even the Pastor at my church had begin to see the the change in me. He'd say Tanya you ready to teach Sunday School, and of course I'd be like no Pastor, thinking he was just joking. But then more of the members began to "call me out". Come on my grandma and all my family been in this this church all these years and y'all barely recognized them. My mom suffered "church hurt", because she just wanted them to accept her. Yeah they knew her story, but they never received her change, they always judged her. Where's the true forgiveness? Mine eyes has seen the glory. So I joined the choir. And that was just the beginning. Because remember I'm one that studies. So I touched on deliverance, demons, tongue speaking. I had no knowledge of the five fold ministry or any of that, but I sought it out. It's my pregnancy I got to feed this baby. It's as if these were my cravings.

Meanwhile Warren has become comfortable again, so now he's back to his old tactics. Stealing my money, using and accusing. All the while I'm trying to be strong. Keeping a smile on my face, whilst I'm crying inside. I couldn't understand why I was going through this? I didn't deserve this. That when God spoke and said "when you find yourself in diverse trials count it all joy". I didn't understand that? What's joyous about this havoc in my home? But I continued to study. Again I visited his mom's church, and now there's a different bond happening with her and I. One we didn't have before. Warren now got the opportunity to drive trucks again, so he starts back working. They never drug tested him, but each time I go to the doctor they tell me I have this chemical or thing in my blood. That's how I know he was doing more than marijuana. He on crack, and it had taken him to a place he had no control of. Even his mother began to notice it. After being on the job for about 9 months, then they tested, he came up positive, and they gave him the boot. At my church I'm doing just what I told the Pastor I couldn't do, I'm teaching Sunday School to the youth, and quickly moving up. They are reconsidering me to be a deaconess. Now that's a special thing in religion. I get to wear my fancy hats, expensive dresses and suits. Yes I accept. "Titles" so I was excited, but they don't understand it wasn't them, it was actually God showing them my spiritual growth. He's the one that "called" me to be a deaconess, teacher, preacher, whatever, not man, I realize that. My teachings didn't line up with what they were used to. They were going by a planned out book which they had been using year in and year out. Never changing. I on the other hand was just allowing Holy Spirit to direct what I spoke about. Yes I had a topic and a notes, but I wouldn't grieve the Holy Spirit. Some of the kids didn't know John 3:16, Psalms 23, Matthew 6:9-16. Really these are the basics in Prayer, so I took it upon myself to teach them to pray these. Prayer is a weapon. They didn't agree with what I was doing or my method. Mine eyes has seen the glory, It wasn't them, the Bible declares we wrestle not against flesh and blood but powers of darkness in heavenly places. God was revealing my place and His purpose for my life and satan didn't like that. So he put all these distractions in the way, Warren, seizures, finances, etc. but I progressed on to now carrying the mantle.

7

CARRYING THE MANTLE

Intro

At this point you'd probably say you've arrived. But I've have to agree with the Apostle Paul, when he says "not that I have already obtained all this or have arrived at my goal, but I press on to take hold of that for which Christ took hold of me. And I strain to press on towards the mark of the higher calling of God in Jesus. Making sure I leave what's behind, behind. You see here is the place where many of us get it wrong. I've discovered that Jesus "called" me, and "chose" me. I've even acted in it prematurely. At the face of trials, I sometimes prevail, but then there are sometimes I cant. Why? Because I'm still playing with God. Not all the way in. Saying yes, but not realizing that my yes comes with consequences. To whom much is given, much is required.

Warren is becoming to be like that thorn in my flesh, and though I've prayed ova and ova and again for God to remove Him, it wont budge. God's grace is sufficient for me. On a cool evening as I look out at the stars I realize this mantle isn't about me its about Jesus. I quickly was set free from one thing and found myself in another. What? Yeah, I left Warren finally. I decided to be real and trust God all the way. Not caring about where I was going, knowing my God would supply all my needs. I tell you the strength you gain by depending solely on Jesus is unmeasurable, because He said in your weakness He is your strength. I gave up myself. Stop smoking cigarettes. Oh yeah you haven't heard of me mentioning a seizure, I haven't had one in a long while. Thank you Jesus. So I lived with my mom for about 2wks, then I had to go to shelter. Call it pride. I don't want nobody saying they did nothing for me, or that I owe them something. The shelter was an easier choice. Flesh speaking. Meanwhile I'm still going to church and my study is more intense. I'm even utilizing the gift and talents God gave me. But I learned, not to fight the devil in flesh, you are setting yourself up for doom. Take it from me I did it. And when satan spanks your butt, it don't feel like when your momma did it. He ain't got no sympathy, love, or passion. He doing it to physically hurt you. To kill you, to destroy you. In the beginning I said "my goal was to reach what God/Jesus already obtained for me. I had to put away what I thought I knew. My prayers had to change. I had to establish an intimate relationship with Christ to the point that I know He wouldn't let me down. As I'm here in the shelter, I again let my fleshly needs ands desires rise up. And I get involved with a man that said he believed what I was doing was good. He understood that it was Glorifying God, but on the other hand he jealous of the time I spend with God, and being about my Father's business. God revealed to me some things while in the shelter. I might've been frightened, but I guess if its your assignment you take to like a duck to water. But first you must loose your downing feathers. I saw me operating a women's ministry, I saw me preaching, I saw me helping those less fortunate than myself (missionary) and God said this what you've been doing all your life. Now its time for you to walk it out. I tell you at that moment I felt like both Jonah and Moses put together, imagine that. I wanted to go forth, but where he wanted me to go I felt was a waste of time. I felt as Jonah did but with shouts of grateful praise, I will sacrifice to you. what I vowed, I will make good. I will say Salvation cometh from the Lord. Not Me? Also I felt like Phoebe and Priscilla all rolled in one. God was using me to speak into many peoples lives and I didn't understand how I was doing it. But I realize, it was the mantle I am carrying, Ma's. Now I've committed to learn everything I need to know about what God's doing through me, and God said "its not you, but he that's in you that is doing all that needs to be done. I just need you to surrender completely. And yeah I said it, but did I mean it? You see God will show your true self.

Soon we get an apartment together, me and the guy I met in the shelter. Living in this house with dude and he put his hands on me. Now I could've easily reacted in a very non-Christian like manner, but I just politely said just take me to my mother's house. What you didn't get angry or upset? No I saw it for just what it was, a distraction. Now I'm in 10th grade in the spiritual realm, and at this stage a lot of things you went through in your elementary, and junior stages are going to be repeated to make sure that the passing grade you acquired you deserve. I see here that I truly did pass this test of self-control. I know it'll come around again but each time the percentage of the grade will be higher and higher. Besides, this was my opportunity to allow God to place the man he chose for me in my pathway.

So I just focus on studying like directed in 2 Timothy 2:15, and put my attention on ministering in non-traditional ways as God leads me. I'm now a Mary Kay consultant, and I tell you God is good. It's like every woman I ran across, was gifted and "called" to help build God's Kingdom. Sometimes I'd set out to go on appointments and get on the bus and say ok Jesus, send me where you want me to go. Be careful what you Pray for........one particular day I prayed this and he said get on the bus and wait for my instructions, so I did. Usually on the metro bus you cant play the music loud, as to not offend anybody. I didn't know this at first.

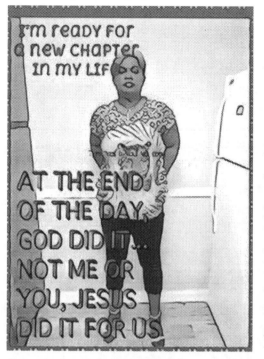

How I discovered this as I had on my head phones but they didn't work, so I said I need my worship music, so I turned the volume to what I thought was low and allowed the music to play. The bus driver says to me, Ma'am you cant play your music so everyone can hear it. But the bus patrons disagreed with that, they were into the music, they had started participated in the worship. Then it gets better. The Holy Spirit said now a mother and a daughter is about to board the bus, and I just want you to be cordial, show the mom the Love of Christ. What? Several mom and daughter duo's got on, but when this particular duo boarded I felt Holy Spirit come over me. So I struck up a conversation with the mom. Mind you the worship music has now taken over the bus. So everyone that gets on is subject to listening to it. The bus driver tried to stop it. The mom said she needed to hear from the Lord and in one of the songs being played she did. You see, she was loosing hope, and

her faith was dwindling. And she had cried to God, and he used me, he uses us or should I say he plants us where he needs us. Now it wasn't just her but there was a Pastor on the bus that needed to be encouraged in the Lord. There was a couple that needed prayer. And all I could say was Use me Lord. I tell you we had church on that bus. I had no idea where I was going, nor how long I was going to be on the bus. I just was being obedient. In that somebody was saved, returned, and touched and agreed with prayers of the people. I've never done this before, but I'd come to realize that church isn't in the four walls, neither is the ministry God is calling me to. So I'm not just teaching I'm ministering and vice a versa, this is only done by a living example...

I come into contact with my first "spiritual mother", some may say she was just a "midwife", but I beg to differ. It was a daunting and cumbersome way of our meeting, it was at my cousin's funeral. She gave his Eulogy, and instantaneously I knew she was the one. Almost like love at first sight. I'd never laid eyes on her before, but the moment I did it was like Elizabeth's baby lept when it came in contact with Jesus while she was pregnant with baby John "The Baptist". My "spiritual baby" lept, and I had to find out who she was? Upon doing so, she invited me to an upcoming program she was having at her church, and of course I attended. I'm nosey, curious, and and anxious all at the same time. But when I arrived something started happening. God stirred up, woke up some things I never knew were there. Mind you we had an upcoming event at our church and they asked me to pick the speaker, so undoubtably I chose her. Now the of the reception of the message not received, it was foreign to them, because in the beginning it was to me as well. But it was confirmation for me, that it was time for me to move on.

After about 2weeks later one of the Associate Pastors started calling me "demon chaser" and Pastor, called me "Reverend", they are seeing it too, it's time to go and so I did. Yeah I left the Big White Hat Society. A change was taking place, while I was in my "quiet time" I heard The Lord say, you shall receive my promises if you don't get slothful. Now Jesus placed the love of my life in my pathway...

I'm working about a week after Father's Day, so I need to get rid of my left over inventory from Mary Kay and here he comes. I had no intentions of being courted, I was working, so when he approached me, I just treated him like a customer and handed him a business card. I had heard about this movie "War Room" and I just had to have it. So after giving him my card, I rushed to find it, but to no avail. He picked up on my disappointment and promised to get it for me, talking about coming to my rescue in my time of need. The thing is he too was searching for the same movie....look at God. This mantle is not light, it is very heavy and only those that are very strong can carry it. But let me help you understand, the moment you say "yes I'll carry it Lord, the devil is right there to try and make you renounce what you said and throw it down. But like those who went before me, I placed my hands in Jesus' and said "carry me as I carry it." Now this mantle isn't to be taken lightly. Sometimes it will get hard. But the Bible tells us to be ready in season and out of season. So back to "my love", I didn't hear from him again for about 1 or 2 months, so I just left it alone. I'd said I'm not "chasing after" nobody, if this is God ordained he will pursue me. Besides the Bible declares it to be so, when a man finds a wife, not the other way around...I was tired of being somebody's girl, lady, boo, and all those other "pet names for a woman used by a man" besides wife.....

Let me caution you, once you decided to walk out your destiny expect trouble on every side. My knowledge and understanding is now progressed what I was taught in my old church, I'm saying too myself "you have to uproot and leave, everything as Paul did. Now I understand why my "spiritual mother" came into my life at that time. She had to help me to birth that. Change, she would be the first to show me what I was "called" to do. And she did just that. I attended a few of her services, and The Holy Spirit said, this is your training ground, so in obedience I joined her congregation. My Pastor says to me as I'm leaving "I already knew this was coming, but the best is yet to come, my mom came with me.....

Tell me God ain't good. I'm reminded of the scripture where God told Moses in (Exodus 4:12, NLT) ("Now go, I will be with you as you speak, and I will instruct you in what to say".

But I have to admit I didn't always allow God to be first, or let me rephrase that go ahead of me. You see now I know I've been called, I know I'm gifted, and I know I'm being used, but I did just what the (Romans 12:3, NET) tells us not to do, and the price is a costly one. Because first of all you think you got it all together not realizing that you're not ready for this type of fight. And believe me the devil loves to attack people that are haughty and prideful, because they are easily to be persuaded. And satan know the word too. And he know that God despises pridefulness. So if you're operating in this manner you're not operating under the anointing, which makes you vulnerable to satan's attacks and tactics. Secondly, God did not send you, so you just went under the assumption of "this is what I supposed to do." Which means you not only jeopardized your life, but the people who came in contact with you. You see, I had to quickly learn to step back and wait, because warfare at this magnitude is not for amateurs.

Again I meet up with my love we go on our first date, to Starbucks, and just sit and talk, at the end of our conversation he says "God told me you're my wife." Yeah just like that he asked me, or should I say he "declared" I was his wife.

The Robbins

Wait a minute brother, pump your brakes, you don't know me like that, and I definitely don't know you, was my inner thought. But outwardly I was thinking, when God is in it you can't do nothin about it. Afterward we went for a stroll in the park and he dropped me off at my my mom's house. She says to me as soon as I get in the door "Tanya you sure you should be getting involved with anybody at this time? I tell you my exact words to her were, he's not just anybody, he's my husband, yeah Holy Spirit confirmed it right then and there. We continue seeing each other and about a month later I invited him to come to my church. I needed to see where his faith level was. And he agreed. All while in church, he telling everybody I'm his wife, and my Pastor asking me when did I get married, I said I didn't but I will. But remember

I haven't mentioned no seizures but on this Sunday while in church I have one, I guess to see if he was going to run or if he was going to stay. I never told him anything about my seizures, didn't have the opportunity to. But lo and behold he stayed. I told you this mantle will be tested over and and over again. Now after I've recuperated he suggests I come live with him. I'm living with mom at this present, because of the last fool. So I politely brush the conversation off. I'm not doing that again. Um um, so another couple days go by, and it's close to Halloween and he poses the question again, I briefly gasp and say "let me think about it, hoping it would take his mind off of the request/question. We go on a date that Saturday it was a beautiful sun a blazing as we walked through the park. We went on a picnic and enjoyed a nice sip of red wine, it was if my love "Wilfred", knew I was going to finally say yes. So we're celebrating in advanced. By the end of the date, he asked again, so I say yeah for a trial run. Mind you this one here he was different. He done took me on a picnic. He brings me flowers every week (12 long stem roses). He opens doors for me, it doesn't matter if it's the car or building a door is a door. Chivalry isn't dead. Did I forget to mention that he is even nice to mom, whatever she needs he is trying to supply.

So the day of the move come, and we're getting all things together and momma cautions me "remember the last one and be be careful", and I said I'm good, and I gave her a kiss and left. Now my departure wasn't normal, I ran down the stairs, as a child being free from the grips of their parents, but I was running into the arms of my husband. We arrive at his place and he had it decked out for a bachelor and he says to me "baby whatever you want to change do so, this is your house. Remember I told you that you would be tested again. Well I didn't know that the place where he lived, we had to share the bathroom and kitchen. I mean come on I left my momma house for this. But then I was reminded, you did it in the shelters and you were good. But the difference here is there is no time limit on how long you shower. You have the luxury of cooking your own food. So I said ok Lord, again I passed the test. Because I'm grateful for these little things and I'm gonna be a good steward over it. But the thing that struck me as odd was one day while showering The Holy Spirit spoke to me and said you're his "First Lady". What, say that again, and he did, you are his "First Lady". Meaning he's a man of clergy, then I immediately start calling him by the nickname "Pastor", yeah I was being quirky not knowing this what God had already ordained. That's what attracted me to him the Jesus in him, not his money, or his car, even though these are two of the things he pointed out to me. He showed me the money in his wallet along with all his credit cards and checks, and then he pointed to his nice automobile, and even told me about his magnificent job, but me I'm not moved by that. Which was why I just handed him a business card. I tell you this wedding process went off so fast. November rolled around and we went up to Jacksonville to visit his daughter, and to get her approval, and she not only approved, but she blessed me with my wedding gown. Because we were trying to figure something out. How are we gonna do this? Where are we gonna do this? How we gonna pay for this? But let me say this, her husband also blessed "Wilfred" with his suit. Work it Jesus. We attended couples counseling and my church leaders were astonished by how soon he'd included me into his finances. They declared upon our second session that is so, yes we are ready to married one to another, in Holy matrimony. Remember I said if God is in it ain't nothin nobody can do. December 6, 2015 after regular service I married the love of my life, Wilfred Lorenzo Robbins and I became Tanyka Lawon Robbins, oh the bliss!

Let me tell you the enemy saw this connection, matrimonial union, and he was both angry and terrified at the same time. I tell you, because we never really knew each other, but those few months. The enemy knows that two of us coming into our fullness would cause him total disfunction, so he knows he must go before us.

Wilfred has a calling on his life, and I too have one, but we both are walking in them slowly. So nonetheless, the devil is speaking into both of our ears. Bringing up pass relationships, trying to point out comparison. Even went as far as to have us in our first year of marriage to separate, thinking we made a mistake. But God don't make no mistakes. The devil is afraid of me coming into my full potential and bringing my husband into his calling, so he tried to bring strife between us. So we stayed separated for about three months, in which he decided to move on. But I had been forewarned by Holy Spirit that "I was his First Lady", so I couldn't disobey what God had named me, it's part of my mantle. So we got back together, I forgave him, it's a part of my mantle. I mean insecurity is a dangerous thing. And if I let the devil drive the train he'll push it (insecurity) into overdrive. Especially when someone who's dealing with and has dealt with insecurity issues. Here I should be fixated on the problems in my marriage not ministry. And I put up a front like I was good, but God knew the truth. Like I say sometimes this mantle gets heavy. But even ones who carry mantles have to realize when it gets heavy lay it aside, release the load, the pressure, and you do that by giving it to Jesus. As soon as I did that I felt a sense of release and relief and I realized that Wilfred was working from a place of fear. He'd never been married to a woman like me, I often time remind him, "you prayed for me, and you found/ sought me".

The next year we move into a bigger place, because my husband says my wife only deserves the best. A man has to go out there and get it from the sweat. I have to provide for my household, these are things I've never heard a man say regarding me and a relationship. Oh yeah, this is more than a relationship it's a marriage ordained by God, so of course the devil is gonna oppose it. We both, my husband and I came to realize that separately we're powerhouses but together we're dynamite, tearing down the kingdom of satan, and that's what he's afraid of, me and my husband touching and agreeing because the word says "where two or three touch and agree, there I am in the midst. Jesus being in our midst means the presence of God, which brings JOY, the fullness of JOY, called liberty, and when the Son makes you free you are free indeed. You see this mantle ain't just for me, but it's for those connected to me. Like any other marriage, we've had our ups and downs, but in the midst of it all we've stayed strong. We separated again in our third year due to me just being sick and tired of being falsely accused. But it wasn't my husband really it was the accuser of the brethren, using my husband. So I decided to cancel that assignment. So I left and went to a women's shelter. Again God is preparing me for things to come. Even there in the shelter, God's mandate has precedence, who God joined together let no man put asunder, not even the two he joined together. While at the shelter I got sick, yeah I have a seizure but it wipes me out for a period and he was my only point of contact. So one of the women call him and, he pick me up take me to the emergency room, and then back home to nurse me back to health. God said I was his First Lady. Even while I was at the shelter I was still about my Father's business, I ministered to the women and caused several to resubmit themselves to Christ. One woman even searched for me every night to make sure we have bible study and prayer before we went to bed and though the staff tried to stop it, you can't stop the flow of God. Even they eventually came to expect it. I last heard that she had returned back to her church and is clean and sober and is an active witness of God's Glory. Meanwhile God is using me to reach out to the people via social media, so the ministry he put me in charge over "I'm not Ashamed of the Gospel of Jesus Christ Women's Ministry can be seen all over YouTube, Facebook, Twitter, WhatsApp, Instagram, and the like. So I'm doing what God called me to do.

I'm at the point now that my studying has revealed to me not only about Him Keeping me thus far, but revealing why He Kept me. This mantle will continue to be mine to carry everyday of my life. Lest I not complete this section with this. I lost my mom, and on the very day of her funeral, during the repast my husband got belligerent and demanding. Family from all over was there and we are all mourning mom's death. But they already had secret intentions. I had no idea of their precepts. So when he acted this way they immediately went into attack mode, which would be anybody's reaction for their loved ones. But they were working under false pretenses. You see earlier in the year I being the thespian that I am had just finished performing and had gone home and decided to iron my husband's work clothes. But before I did that I did a Facebook live, anyhow, whilst I was ironing I had a seizure and the scorching hot water burned my skin causing abrasions I didn't know were there. When I did I went to the emergency room, called mom, and from that point on they believed he was physically abusing me. Besides some of the things he was getting away with doing and saying to me, nobody ever had liberty to treat me this way. So they believed I was afraid of him, nonetheless the mantle that I carry says "I am his First Lady", that's why he got away with it. The covenant I made with him and God. So to keep the peace I stayed with the family, and they convinced almost demanded that I leave him. So I thought long and not so much as hard. I tell you this thing is heavy, and it can't be thrown away. I left my husband again for a third time for four months, to get some breathing room, direction, and instruction from God. And God brought us back together. But I realized its under this mantle is the covering of grace, in this mantle is God's power, by this mantle comes wisdom, for this mantle is love of God. So yes I'll carry the mantle given to me by Christ and I will run this race with patience. Because God is in control of every obstacle that arises. It is being placed in my pathway not to trip me up but to keep me aware and build me up. So I'll never let down my guard. I hope that throughout this book you've discovered that Jesus didn't leave you because you're facing trials, he kept you so that while you're facing those trials, you'll count it all joy, you'll turn to Him and let Him lead you.

8

REFLECTIONS, PRAYERS, ENCOURAGEMENT

Salvation- my receipt reads paid in full not pending nor declined. (Galatians 3:13-14 DRB) us from the curse of the law, having become a curse for us. That the blessing of Abraham might come upon the Gentiles in Jesus Christ, that we might receive the promise of the Spirit through faith.

The blood of Jesus was used to pay the cost for us. Our salvation and total victory in Christ Jesus is itemized as the cost was death, the payment was the blood of Jesus.

Date: over 2000 years ago

1. Healing	2. Deliverance
3. Sins.	4. Forgiveness
5. Peace.	6. Joy
7. Marriage	8. Protection
9. Redemption	10. Ministry
11. Family.	12. Life

Total number of items: 12

Total price: Death
Payment rendered
The Blood Of Jesus

Change
Eternal Life
Please Retain For Your Records
Store: Calvary

So never let the enemy say to you that you owe him nothin. The debt is settled. PAID IN FULL, BY THE BLOOD OF JESUS. He'll try to trick you into trying to repay, but realize it cannot happen.

Father I thank you for paying my debts in full. I know that I could never repay you, so I'll continue to be forever grateful and praise you. Help me to live a life according to your payment, and that's full total and completed in Jesus. Amen.

He kept me words of power.......(vocabulary words)

1. Mirror- reflects truth (2 Corinthians 3:18 AMP) being transformed continuously means growing daily, this is Gods way of progression. We need to let God kill what's causing us to stay in regress so that we can progress. This comes through The Holy Spirit. Look at yourself today, now you declare I'm dying to me, yet I'm alive in Christ by The Holy Spirit.

2. Counsel- judgement and accountability (Proverbs 19:20-21, BSB) Listen, pay attention, give an ear to counsel. Let it redirect your footsteps. Gods plans for your life requires His wisdom that only comes from Him. At many times we face situations were not sure are good, so we ask people's opinions. Let God direct you, so that He's the only one to speak into your future. He has the plan already mapped out (Jeremiah 29:11), let Him guide you through His counsel which is The Word, The Bible.

3. Preparation/Exercise- (Romans 5:1-6 ESV) here we come to a place where we must use our faith to get us to the next level. Trusting that God's tests in our lives are ordained by Him. Putting into practice our patience which produces our Godly character. As often as you are tried just know you are prepared twice as much. God gives us double, remember we serve a God of abundance in our faith. Preparation is your confirmation that God's favor is upon you. Use it. Put it to work. Everything you need to live a Holy and righteous life God has already given you.

4. Zeal- (1 Kings 19:9-10 NAS) be zealous for Jesus. Let your motivation bring you to a place of total surrender. Devote yourself to the work of the Lord. Never be too busy for Jesus. The same time and energy you're putting into the cares of this world, put double into Jesus. Be over zealous. This is showing that no matter what I will be about My Father's Business. This gets you to the point of victory.

5. Lesson- (Matthew 18:3 KJV) many lessons come to show you your strengths and your weaknesses. The power in this word lesson is maturity and growth. Learn through everything trust God, as you forever learn and grow.

Get familiar with these words and their meaning in your journey as you are in Christ. These words will be used repeatedly in life both naturally and spiritually but because of the preceding words of power you're able to operate in them. Because you know the truth from the "mirror", and you're accountable through "counsel", to show your faithfulness because of "preparation". You've been tested in your devotion through "zealous" actions, of the "lessons" in life which produced growth, so now you too can declare and know HE KEPT YOU.

Daily Devotional Words

1. Wisdom- (Proverbs 4:7-9 ESV) seek the wisdom of God and you will be able to make decisions that are pleasing to Him, and they will guide you into all truth. Holy Spirit will be your empowerment for this type of wisdom. Ask God to give you His wisdom today.

2. Faith- (Hebrews 11:1 NIV) faith comes as we hear God speaking to our spirits. Many times we can't understand what drives us to act, but if we just let God lead and trust in Him all the way, we will prevail. Faith is confidence in the things unknown, but willing to do it anyway. This is what we need in times of confusion. Faith gives us the peace we seek. Ask God for Unwavering Faith today.

3. Peace-(Philippians 4:7 NIV) this is complete confidence in God's ability to meet your need at every given moment. It works because you trust Him, and you've given Him your entire life. Be the one that know when I call Jesus, He'll be there. No matter what I can count on Jesus to come through. This kind of peace will get you to the next level in Christ. Ask Him for His peace today.

4. Love-(John3:16 NIV) tells you that God loves you so much that He gave you His best. So that you can have The Best. The love of God produces love. When you live in God's love, nothing else has priority, because you know that God is your everything. God's love does not judge you for the things you do, but it accepts you for who you are. God's love teaches you to trust Him, it shows His faithfulness to you. You're special to God and He loves you. Receive God's love today.

5. Hope-(Psalms 71:5 NIV) Jesus is our hope. As we trust in Him we will see the manifestation of the promises of God. Being confident in Jesus' ability to do just what He says He's going to do is hope. Do you have this type of Hope? Ask God for hope today? Live in it, for by it comes faith which pleases God. Which now you're in position to lean on Jesus. Receive the certain hope of Jesus today.

6. Joy-(Psalms16:11 NIV) the way to life is God's presence. Here awaits complete total joy. Where there is joy, peace abides as well. Love is dwelling there too. Joy causes us to make wise decisions through Devine Guidance and Counsel. Ask God for the joy of The Lord to be yours today.

7. Forgiveness-(Luke 23:24 NIV) forgiveness is an unselfish act of love. Asking Our Father to forgive us is a way of showing love and confidence to God. Jesus says they don't know what they are doing. Though many people hurt harm or endanger you, understand that they are pushing, catapulting, you into the arms of Jesus. Forgiveness is pardoning, canceling, releasing, remitting a debt. Jesus has empowered you to forgive. Forgiveness is the power tool needed for you to become whole. Jesus forgave you, so forgive those or them today.

8. Power-(Ephesians 3:20 NIV) This power is the same power that raised Jesus from the dead, it's called The Holy Spirit. When we speak of Power of God there are 3.
   {1 Dunamis- miracle working ability
   2 Exousia- authority
   3 Kratos- strength
   God's power is what activates our spirit. This power is a promise from God. Receive God's Power today.

9. Endurance- (James 5:11 ERV) endurance is the ability to exert yourself for long periods of time. First of all its a trait of the fruit of the spirit. Spiritual Endurance is a mark of a victorious Christian. Through life's difficult times it's the display of hope and faith in Jesus. Being confident that the presence of The Lord is with you. It's ongoing. Endurance is the guarantee that nothing can ever influence your personal relationship with Jesus. Ask God for Spiritual Endurance today.

10. Strength-(2 Corinthians 12:9-10 GNB) Jesus promises that His Grace will keep you in your time of weakness, therefore welcome your hardships, persecutions, trials, and difficulties. It's Here we'll discover our true strength is being dependent on Jesus. Jesus has empowered you with The Holy Spirit, so you will always be strong. Your flesh may grow weak, but your spirit will be strong forever. Ask God for continued strength today.

11. Boldness- (Acts 4:29-31 ERV) even through your obedience to Jesus know that people will say what you are not and can not be or do. But just continue proclaiming Jesus as Your Lord and Savior. Speak in the authority given to you by Jesus. Being bold requires confidence in "The Truth". While being strengthened be sensitive to the people and speak with gentleness and respect. Ask God for boldness today, then use it to win souls for Christ.

12. Courage- (Deuteronomy 31:6 NKJV) this courage enhances your confidence in Jesus. Because you know He is always present. When adversity arises you can face it without fear. Courage puts you where you "can" be used by Jesus. Ask God to give you relentless courage today, it's time rise up now.

13. Grateful- (Hebrews 12:28 NET) worship God at all times giving Him thanks for who He is. Thank God for The Kingdom of God. To be grateful requires us to reflect back

on ourselves and look at where we were and where we are now, and give God Praise. To be grateful is to realize that God's love is unconditional and give Him thanks. Tell God I'm grateful today.

14. Holiness- (1 Peter 1:15-16 NLT) holiness is a way of life. We as children of God should conduct ourselves accordingly. After all we represent God who is Holy. Everything you do is being recorded in The Lambs Book of Life, and when Jesus returns that will be the determining factor of you entering into Heaven. For the Bible declares without holiness no one will see the Lord. Today is your opportunity to receive holiness. Ask God to give you holiness. Ask Him to make you Holy, so that you can be known as His sacred treasure.

15. Mercy- (Lamentations 3:22-23 NLT) God's mercy is renewed everyday. We don't deserve it, but He give it despite our flaws. God's mercy is a cleanser for our souls. God desires mercy. He wants us to love Him with all our hearts, mind, and soul. Give somebody mercy today. Blessed is the merciful for they shall obtain mercy. Thank God for His Mercy. Receive God's mercy today.

16. Knowledge- (1 Corinthians 13:9-12 NLT) knowledge is a sign of spiritual maturity. As we grow in grace we grow in knowledge. Knowledge is used to make Godly decisions. The things you knew before was training or should I say preparation to the ending God has for you. Ask God to give you the knowledge to make Godly decisions. Knowledge to discover goodness in the Lord.

What must I do to be saved?

This part of the book is for all who want a personal relationship with Jesus. It is through this process that you will secure your place in Heaven.

This must be done voluntarily, and if you are ready to receive Jesus follow these steps.

1. Those that "call" on the the name of The Lord shall be saved.

Romans 10:9-10(GNT) says, v9 if you confess that Jesus is Lord and believe that God raised Him from the dead, you will be saved. v10 For it's by your faith that you are put right (redeemed) unto a God. It is by your confession that you are saved.

2. Pray- Dear God, I know I am a sinner, and I ask for your forgiveness. I believe Jesus Christ is your son, and you raised him from the dead. I want to trust him as my Savior and follow him as my Lord, from this day forward, guide my life and help me to do your will. I pray this in Jesus name Amen

If you prayed this prayer in sincerity you are now saved!!!! HALLELUJAH

Now think about visiting and joining a local church near you, and allow the Holy Spirit to lead from now forth into all God has for you.

WELCOME TO THE FAMILY

 May the Lord Bless you and keep you. May the Lord make His face to smile upon you, and be gracious to you. And may God give you peace in your going out and coming in, in your lying down or your rising up, in your labor, and in your leisure, in your laughter and in your tears. Until you come to stand before Jesus in that day in which there is no sunset and no dawning in the name of Father, Son, and Holy Spirit. Amen.

The devil thought he had me, but I go away, GOD GLORY BE TO

Evangelist Tanyka L Robbins

Printed in the United States
by Baker & Taylor Publisher Services